Understanding Other People

by Stuart Palmer

9780449308158

A Premier Book
Fawcett Publications, Inc., Greenwich, Conn.

To Anne

A Premier Book published by arrangement with
Thomas Y. Crowell Company

Copyright MCMLV, Stuart Palmer.
All rights reserved, including the right to reproduce
this book or portions thereof.

Third Premier printing, May 1961

All characters in this book are fictional and
any resemblance to persons living or dead
is purely coincidental.

Premier Books are published by Fawcett World Library,
67 West 44th Street, New York 36, New York
Printed in the United States of America

WORRIER ... BOASTER ... HE-MAN AND GLAMOR GIRL ... WIFE BEATER ... SOCIAL CLIMBER ... OVEREATER ... PERFECTIONIST ... SEX MANIAC ... RECLUSE ...

These "types" are among your friends, associates, neighbors, relatives.

What made some of them withdraw to the sidelines of life? What made others over-aggressive? What made some too anxious to be liked—others desperately avoid dislike?

The people of Madison, Stuart Palmer's imaginary town, are characteristic of people everywhere. From learning to understand their motivations, you will know better how to get along with people like them ... and how better to understand yourself.

Premier Books are designed to bring to a larger reading public books which were formerly available only at a much higher cost

PREFACE

THIS BOOK attempts to explain, in nonscientific language, the reasons behind the various behavior patterns, the various habits, of people in everyday life. Obviously, it does not have all the answers. Human behavior is the epitome of complexity and all the answers are not known. Nonetheless, much is known which can be of help in understanding the behavior of our neighbors, friends, passing acquaintances and even, perhaps, of ourselves.

The system of explanation used here is, in the over-all sense, purely my own. But in its parts it draws widely on the theories, concepts, and generalizations of psychology, sociology, and cultural anthropology, all of which are concerned with explaining human behavior. The system used assumes that the behavior of an individual is always a response to a need and it holds that most behavior is learned.

As its specific point of departure this system takes the Law of Effect of the great psychologist, Thorndike. This Law of Effect can be interpreted as follows: When a particular act by an individual leads to satisfaction of one or more of his needs, that act tends to be learned, to become a habit, a pattern of behavior, which will be used in the future. Conversely, when an act leads to frustration of one or more needs, it does not tend to be learned but, rather, it tends to be avoided in the future.

Taking this law as its point of departure, the explanatory system used here is, in brief, as follows: There are two related needs, both learned by the individual in early childhood, which frequently demand satisfaction and toward which much behavior in modern society is directed; these are the needs for the approval of other people and for avoiding the disapproval of other people. The particular behavior which a given individual uses to satisfy these needs will tend to be that which, because of the specific nature of his past environment, especially of his childhood environment, has proved most effective.

But, at times and because of adverse past environmental circumstances, the individual will not have been able to learn any effective behavior for satisfying either his need for approval or for avoiding disapproval. When this is the case the individual feels frustrated and a third need, the inborn need to aggress, automatically arises and demands satisfaction. The way in which the individual tries to satisfy this need to aggress will depend, again, on the nature of his past environment.

Using this basic explanatory scheme and various ramifications of it, I have attempted to explain the reasons behind fifty different behavior patterns which are more or less common in modern society. To do this, I have imagined a typical, small city called Madison and I have drawn sketches of fifty of its inhabitants in action, each of whom follows one of these patterns in much of his behavior. These are fictional characters intended to be representative of many people who exhibit the behavior in question; as such, they are not sketches of specific, living persons. In each case only the reasons for the particular behavior pattern which the character's actions typify are explained.

We are centrally concerned here with the reasons behind distinctive behavior patterns, rather than with explaining total personalities. This is why the psychoanalytic theories and concepts of Freud and those who came after him are seldom referred to explicitly. The latter are concerned with the infinitely involved matter of plumbing the depths of total personalities.

It almost goes without saying that our emphasis on behavior patterns rather than total personalities leads to some oversimplification. When behavior is analyzed without considering fully the context of the personality in which it is rooted, oversimplification is inevitable. However, simplification, even oversimplification, is often the necessary first step toward understanding.

STUART PALMER

CONTENTS

1 INTRODUCTION: THE PEOPLE OF MADISON ... 13

PART I APPROVAL

2 LIMELIGHTERS ... 21
Attention-Getter · Boaster · He-Man and Glamor Girl

3 END RUNNERS AND LONG-RANGERS ... 32
Self-Deprecating · Liar · Social Climber · Overworker

4 CONSTRUCTIVES ... 48
Creative · Philanthropist · Kind

PART II APPROVAL AND DISAPPROVAL

5 VERBAL EXTREMISTS ... 59
Two Talkers · Enigmatic

6 SELF-IMPRESSED ... 67
Pompous · Snob · Pseudo-Intellectual

7 OVERDOERS ... 78
Self-Righteous · Reformer · Scrupulously Honest · Do-Gooder

PART III DISAPPROVAL

8	SIDELINERS *Shy · Recluse · Lazy*	92
9	POOR AVOIDERS *Worrier · Indecisive · Chain-Smoker · Overeater · Psychosomatic*	101
10	ODD AVOIDERS *Phobic · Perfectionist*	111
11	ESCAPISTS *Alcoholic · Homosexual*	121

PART IV AGGRESSION, APPROVAL AND DISAPPROVAL

12	VERBALIZERS *Arguer · Complainer · Gossip · Disquieting*	133
13	LAWBREAKERS *Juvenile Delinquent · Two Thieves*	146
14	KILLERS *Murderer · Suicide*	157
15	HUMOROUS AND OTHERWISE *Humorous · Petty Officious · Race-Hater · Jealous · Bombastic*	166

PART V AGGRESSION

16	EXTREMISTS *Rapist · Sadist · Arsonist*	184
17	SMALLTIMERS *Surly · Poor-Loser · Wife-Beater*	196
18	A CONCLUDING WORD	205

Understanding
Other People

Chapter 1

INTRODUCTION: THE PEOPLE OF MADISON

THERE IS a quiet man living in the small city of Madison who beats his wife quite thoroughly and regularly. About once a month attacks of rage come over him and he loses all control of himself. His wife is a prim, quiet, little black-and-blue woman. By occupation he is the manager of a book and stationery store. He seems like a pleasant enough sort when you meet him on the street. Yet a short while ago he went to extremes and tried to stick his wife in the furnace. Fortunately she would not fit. Why does he persist in doing this sort of thing?

Then there is a young married woman who has an uncontrollable fear of crowds. She cannot go into cities or any crowded place; she panics. Why does this overwhelming fear come over her when she is among a group of strangers? The one exception is when she is accompanied by her husband. Then she feels vaguely uncomfortable but she can manage. Why is there this one exception?

Why do people do any of the things they do? Why do some people murder and some commit suicide? Why are some people homosexuals and others rapists? Apart from unusual actions, why do people do any of the ordinary things they do? We all know people who talk incessantly; people who become angry over nothing; people who kill you with kindness; and people who offer kindness when you really need it. Why do they act as they do? What are the springs which set off their actions?

We shall try to answer these questions by analyzing the behavior of a number of people who live in a particular place, the city of Madison. . . .

Madison is a small, mythical city with a population of thirty thousand. Actually, it is a cross between a small city and a large semisuburbanized town. Two-thirds of the workers earn their living in Madison and a third commute to the big city and earn it there.

Madison has one long, main business street and a dozen or so secondary business streets. There are three small department stores, some smart shops, many plain shops, several banks, two hotels, a lot of bars and restaurants, and a few cocktail lounges. It is not a particularly pretty street but it is clean.

Several factories are located just off the west end of the main street. Among and around them is Black Row —Madison's slum area. About half of its inhabitants are Negroes and the rest are very poor whites.

Along the streets leading out from the center of town are large frame houses, mostly of the two-family type and forty or fifty years old. They are predominantly grayish-white or tan in color. In early summer some have a few roses out front or to one side. Here live the families of laboring men and of some small businessmen. When one lives here, he lives "right in town." This is not considered a good residential area but it is much better than Black Row, nonetheless.

There are five other residential areas besides the houses right in town and Black Row. At the west end of town out beyond the factories and Black Row are two areas called Breezy Acres and Westville. In each of these, new small houses stand row on row almost as far as the eye can see. The young folks just starting out usually buy a home here.

On the other end of Madison, the east end, is Highland Avenue, a continuation of the main street. The street inclines as it leaves town. Here are the fine old homes of yesterday's wealthy—the higher up the hill you go the finer the homes and the wealthier were their owners—yesterday. Highland Avenue is still considered a fine area of Madison in which to live, but no better than either Beauty Hills or Glenhaven, both of which are nearby.

Beauty Hills is just north of Highland Avenue and Glenhaven is just south of it. In these areas stand medium-sized houses, not too close together, and each with a tree and a stone or brick barbecue behind. Here the well-established middle-class folk dwell. Often the young folks who start out in Westville or Breezy Acres sell their houses there and move to Beauty Hills or Glenhaven when they become established. The new high school and shopping center are close by.

Out beyond Beauty Hills is the Whippoorwill Country Club, most of whose members live in Beauty Hills or Glenhaven. The club has a nine-hole golf course, two weedy tennis courts, and a rambling old clubhouse. It is a place where, as the members say, everybody can get together and have some good clean fun.

South of both Glenhaven and the fine old homes on Highland Avenue is Fairview Manor. This is the top residential area in Madison. Zoning laws forbid the building of houses costing less than thirty thousand dollars. Here live the very financially successful business and professional men of Madison. There are stone pillars at the entrance to Fairview Manor but no armed guards.

To the south of Fairview Manor is the Orange Club, *the* country club of Madison. If you belong to the Orange Club you may put a little sticker with an orange-colored disc on it in the rear window of your car. This is something new put through by some of the younger members. Near the Orange Club is Miss Tooney's Country Day School where matriculate the children of most of the families living in Fairview Manor.

In summary, the wealthiest families of Madison live in Fairview Manor although a few are still left on Highland Avenue. The more successful middle-class people live in Beauty Hills or Glenhaven. The less successful middle-class people and those just starting out live in Breezy Acres or Westville. The laboring men and small businessmen and their families tend to live in the old two-family houses lining the streets right in town, and the poorest whites and the Negroes live in Black Row by the factories.

Madison is a place much like any other, a place where people live and learn. We will try to see why some of the people who live there learn to act as they do.

The simplified system of explanation that we will use takes as its point of departure modern psychological learning theory, which holds that any piece of behavior that leads to reward, to satisfaction of a need, will be learned, will become a habit. Likewise, a person will learn a new, more specific need for the particular reward which satisfied the original need and, often, for whatever happened to be associated with the reward—for whatever was present when it satisfied the individual's original need.

The behavior of the people of Madison and of all people for that matter is always directed toward satisfying needs. If there is no need in the individual, there will be no behavior. Human needs are of two kinds: inborn and learned. People are born with the needs for food, air, excretion, and the like. But as they develop, they learn such needs as those for money or for the approval of other people. And most of the behavior that they use in their attempts to satisfy their needs is learned as well. The particular kinds of needs and the particular kinds of behavior that they learn depend on the nature of their *total past environment* and particularly on the other people who have been a part of it.

At the risk of considerable oversimplification, it can be said, it seems to me, that much of the behavior of the people of Madison and of most people in modern society is directed toward satisfying one or more of *three* broad types of needs. First, there is behavior directed toward satisfying the learned need for the *approval* of other people. Second, there is behavior directed toward satisfying the learned need to avoid the *disapproval* of other people. Third, there is behavior directed toward satisfying the need *to aggress*; this need to aggress is inborn and arises when one of the other two needs—for approval or to avoid disapproval—has been frustrated. Sometimes, a person's behavior is directed toward satisfying two or even all three of these needs at the same time. The particular type of behavior which a given person learns and uses to try to satisfy these needs will depend upon the nature of his earlier environment.

The three chapters in Part I are concerned with people in Madison who direct much of their behavior toward trying to satisfy their need for approval. The chapters in Parts II through V are concerned with people in Madison who direct much of their behavior toward trying to satisfy their needs to avoid disapproval or to aggress and, in some cases, their need for approval as well. It should be made clear that when we discuss a given person in this book and say, for example, that his habit of self-deprecation, of running himself down, is really an indirect attempt to satisfy his need for approval, we do not mean that *all* his behavior is directed toward that need. We simply mean that his habit of self-deprecation is so directed. Other behavioral habits of his, which we do not discuss, will often be directed toward satisfying other needs. (Were we to analyze these other habits of his, we would find, however, that they were frequently directed toward satisfying the need to avoid disapproval or the need to aggress.)

Now you will say that it is true that some behavior is directed toward satisfying the needs for approval, for avoiding disapproval, and for aggression. But you will say what about genuinely kind behavior, what about laziness, what about homosexuality or half a hundred other forms of behavior. Well, we shall see. We shall get to them.

And what about yourself, you will say. You don't go around always trying to get approval. You don't bother much about avoiding disapproval. And you certainly aren't aggressive. Well, you are an exception, of course. You and I. I'm an exception, too. I'm talking about everybody else.

PART I

APPROVAL

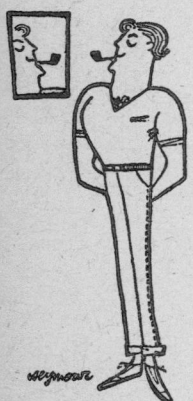

He-Man: He was a startlingly handsome boy ...

Glamor Girl: She suns in the most obvious places ...

APPROVAL is used here in the broadest sense. It includes any action by others which the individual has learned to interpret as indicative of his being well thought of by the society around him. Approval may take the form of admiration, praise, esteem, respect, compliment, affection, or attention. Any action by others which increases the individual's feeling of prestige, of his having a place in the sun, of his being significant falls within the sphere of approval. For those with psychological knowledge, this need for approval is somewhat like Adler's urge for superiority, but it does not have the aggressive aspects of the latter and it is wholly learned while the latter is not.

Learning the need for approval of others begins in the early years of life. It takes place in this way: when the child does what his parents want him to do, they reward him most; they let him have and do what he wants; they give him candy, they let him stay up a little longer and so on. In effect, they are satisfying needs he has for candy and staying up late; these are actual needs which the child has learned and their satisfaction means a lot to him. At the same time that the parents reward the child, they give him approval for having done what they wanted him to do. They pat him on the head and they tell him what a good boy he is. Gradually, the child learns that the approval of his parents goes along with, and stands for, reward. Thus he learns the need for their approval. He learns this in an unconscious way but he learns it nonetheless.

In school, the child's teachers carry on the process. He gradually learns that approval of people in general stands for reward, for satisfaction. Consequently, he develops habits for attempting to gain approval. By the time he is an adult, he directs much of his behavior toward trying to satisfy this learned need for approval. The particular ways in which he directs it depend on what he has been given approval for in his past environment. For example, if his parents have given him approval for being very polite then one of the ways he will try to get approval as an adult is by being very polite. On the other hand, if his parents have given him approval for doing things which are, in effect, impolite then he will try to get approval as an adult by doing those things.

One further point: having learned a need for the approval of others, people go on to learn a need for self-approval. They do so because when other people approve of them they figuratively pat themselves on the back, approve of themselves. Their own approval goes along with, and stands for, the approval of others and so they eventually learn a need for it also.

Chapter 2

LIMELIGHTERS

PEOPLE whose behavior tends to be directed toward gaining approval usually fall into one of three groups. First, there are those who try to gain approval directly by seeking the limelight. Second, there are those who try to gain it by various indirect methods. The third group is really a special group within the second group; it is made up of those people who try to gain approval indirectly through particularly constructive behavior.

In this chapter we'll consider the first group, the most obvious group—the limelighters. The need for approval sticks out all over them. As a result they do not gain much approval. Being obvious about the need for approval—showing off, for example—will not do at all in our society. One must be a little subtle about it. Most people realize this. But there are some, the limelighters, who do not realize it. Or they realize it only partially. They go on trying to get approval directly because their past environment has been such that they have not been able to learn other ways for getting it.

Susan Howard is a good example of this type. Most people in the Beauty Hills section of Madison who know the Howards say it's amazing how Richard Howard puts up with his wife, Susan. They say she spends a small fortune on clothes and she certainly can't afford it, she drinks too much at the club, and her flirting is too obvious. She has a sitter for the baby almost every afternoon; as she says, she has to get out once in a while.

Susan is about thirty and attractive but a little on the thin and drawn side. Her hair is auburn and very long. She makes quite a point of her hair and spends much time arranging it in various ways.

When the Howards went to the Whippoorwill Country Club last Saturday night, Susan was wearing a green Chinese costume decorated with dragons and was looking very mysterious. Her round-faced husband Dick greeted everyone enthusiastically, as usual. Susan walked over to the group of wives. "Why that's a simply stunning dress," Janet Stocker said to her. "We never dreamed you were pregnant again, dear."

"Get me a drink, Dick," Susan called to her husband. She remained standing and took out her cigarette holder. The other wives were talking about the children.

"Well, here we are again," Susan said. "Week in, week out. I wish to God we could discuss something other than diapers." She held out her hand and took the drink from her husband without looking at him.

"What would you suggest?" Janet Stocker said. "The Orient?"

"May I dance with your husband, dear?" Susan said to Janet and left the group to ask Steve Stocker to dance with her. When they finished the dance, Steve, slim and blackhaired, got her a drink.

By midnight Susan was still standing and she was loud. She had taken down her long hair; and, when she wasn't dancing, drinking or squealing, she whirled in a dance step or two by herself. She looked rather odd, gliding about alone with her eyes half closed. She was the center of attention as was usually the case at this time on Saturday night at the Club.

Susan and Steve Stocker danced again, fast, with her dark red hair streaming out behind. When the dance ended they both went down in a heap on the floor. Susan's husband Dick picked her up. Steve Stocker stayed on the floor looking surprised.

"Let's go home now, Sue," Dick said.

"No," Susan said and spun halfway around.

Dick waited and then said, "We ought to go, Sue."

She was looking at the wives who were momentarily making a point of not looking at her. "All right," she said suddenly.

Dick got her coat and they left. Driving home neither spoke.

When they were home Dick said, "Want some coffee, Sue?"

"All right."

Dick made the coffee while Susan sat at the kitchen table. "Sue, are you all right?" Dick said when he brought the coffee. "Feel sick?"

She did not answer him.

"This'll make you feel better."

Susan drank the coffee. She looked as though she were going to cry. "Oh, God," she said, half aloud.

"What's the matter, Sue?" Dick said.

"Leave me alone."

Dick got up, went over to her and put his arm around her shoulder. "What's the matter, Sue?" he said. She didn't say anything. "Tell me what's the matter, Sue."

"Nothing," she said. "Nothing's the matter."

"Come on, Sue. What is it? It'll help to tell me. What's the matter?"

"I said nothing's the matter."

He put his finger under her chin and raised her face. He kissed her forehead.

Susan looked up at him. She looked very young now. "I don't know what's the matter with me, Dick. I don't seem to get along with anyone. No one likes me. I don't know, it's—"

"You'll be all right, Sue. Just a little too much to drink," Dick said.

"No, Dick. There's something wrong with me. I always seem to be searching for something. I try to be different from the others. And I only make a fool of myself doing it. I don't seem to be satisfied with anything. I don't know—" She shook her head.

"Now, Sue. Don't feel that way. We'll be making more money before the year is out and you can—"

"No. It won't make any difference."

"Sure it will, Sue—"

"I wish I were different," Susan said.

Now we all know people like Susan, people who are always trying to be the center of attention. They can't seem to relax and have a good time. They get attention, yes. But in the main they only make fools of themselves while doing it. Their actions only make people dislike them. Sometimes they realize this, as Susan does. But they have a strong need for the approval of others, and getting attention is the only way they have learned for trying to satisfy it. Attention has come to stand for approval. So they go on, clinging to the old attention-getting habits which work only poorly, at best.

As we said, most children learn a need for the approval of others. The mother rewards the child most when she approves of him. In this way approval comes to stand for reward and satisfaction and thus the child learns a need for it.

As a little girl Susan learned a need for approval in this manner. But she also learned from her mother that being the center of attention was the best way to get it. Susan's mother was a woman to whom appearances meant everything. She had attempted to rise in the social sphere of Madison and she had failed. She had failed because of Susan's father. He never achieved any position of real importance in the community. He taught chemistry in the Madison High School and teaching chemistry was his only interest. His position was one of fair prestige but the salary was low. And he had no desire to go further.

Susan's mother often said, "Robert could have been principal and then county superintendent, if only he'd wanted to." But he hadn't wanted to.

When Susan was four, her mother was forty and well frustrated in her desire for social success in Madison. She transferred her ambitions to her daughter. From her mother, Susan learned that being the center of attention was a way of getting approval. She was a beautiful child and her mother would dress her up whenever "lady friends" were coming to call. And they came often.

When the lady friends had arrived her mother would continually approve of Susan's appearance. And she gave the lady friends no choice but to do likewise.

"Susan, come over here and show the ladies your new dress," her mother would say.

Susan would go over and turn slowly within the circle of ladies.

"What a beautiful child, my dear," the ladies would remark.

"You are a lovely child," one would say to Susan.

"I just don't know where she gets it," Susan's mother would say, laughing briefly. Then she would put her arm around Susan and hug her.

This went on and on.

These were the times when Susan usually got approval. Her mother seldom, if ever, approved of her at other times. Being the center of attention was the only thing which led to satisfaction of Susan's need for the approval of others. So, she learned to want to be the center of attention.

When Susan went to school she found of course that she was not automatically the center of attention. She was prettier than most of the other children; and her mother always dressed her in party dresses. But a lot of the time no one paid much attention to her. Yet being the center of attention was the only way she knew to get approval. She took to squealing loudly and with apparent delight for no apparent reason. This drew attention to her but it did not always lead to approval. Sometimes her teachers felt she was just trying to attract attention. However, she was a beautiful child and her dresses were very pretty; also her father taught in the high school. So, frequently her teachers did make a fuss over her. "Just like a beautiful little doll," they sometimes said.

All in all, Susan's attention-getting behavior was quite rewarding. So it continued through grammar school and high school. Of course, she made some enemies because of it. Many of the girls disliked her. But the boys obviously approved of her.

After high school Susan took a job in the semi-exclusive Madison High-style Dress Shop. Her mother liked the idea of her being in an exclusive shop. Her father vaguely wanted her to go to college but Susan knew that if she went to college she would be on a very slim budget and have few clothes. If she went to work at the dress shop she would not only be getting a salary but she could get dresses at cost. She had not learned any long-range habits for getting approval. She could not go without attention-getting clothes for four years. Besides, she had a secret desire to be a model. While she knew she had little chance, her chances were better in the dress shop, all in all.

Susan's attention-getting behavior continued. It had come to the point where she felt anxious if she did not continually attract attention. She bleached her hair blond. She wore the newest and most extreme dresses—one-third off at the dress shop. She still squealed with apparent delight. Several of the girls in the crowd she went around with disapproved of her, thought her "so obviously after attention." But it was apparent that some of them also envied her. And Dick Howard, the round-faced, good-natured boy in the crowd, hung on her every word and act. There was approval in his eyes.

His approval had three effects. Since he was well liked, it kept Susan in the crowd. It rewarded her need for approval. And it caused her to marry Dick, the source of that reward.

The Howards have been married eight years now. They have a two-year-old daughter. And Susan's attention-getting behavior is more extreme than ever. A few of the husbands in Madison's Whippoorwill Country Club set continue to flirt with her. But most of the wives dislike her thoroughly. Susan realizes this. She knows that she is fighting a losing battle, that as time goes on people dislike her more and more. But she doesn't know what to do about it. For her, attention has always stood for approval. Attention-getting is the only habit she has learned for getting approval. It is better than nothing. She can't try some new way of getting approval: she is afraid of making a fool of herself. And so she goes on, tightening the vicious circle of her behavior.

Another type who tries to get approval by throwing the spotlight on himself is the boaster. Like Susan, he too is disapproved of by society because he is too obvious about trying to gain approval. But he is not particularly aware of that. He feels that you are bound to approve of him if he can only tell you of his exploits, which are always considerable, both in quantity and uniqueness.

A goodly number of such persons reside in Madison. A prime example is Lester MacDougal, a frequent guest at cocktail parties.

MacDougal stands baggily tweeded against the door of a living room in Beauty Hills. His last listener has just excused himself rather suddenly and MacDougal is on the alert for a replacement.

A man behind MacDougal says, "Excuse me, please," in an effort to clear the doorway of MacDougal. MacDougal turns, perceives a stranger, and brightens. Out comes the right hand. "I don't believe we've met," MacDougal says. "Name's MacDougal—Mac for short."

The man seems surprised and says, "My name is Peale. Bill Peale. How do you do?"

"Not bad. Not bad at all, for a man who just got back to civilization," answers MacDougal.

Peale looks momentarily confused, then says, "Well, nice to meet you, MacDougal," and starts to move into the room.

"What I mean to say is, I just got back from the nation's capital." MacDougal laughs briefly.

Peale turns back toward him. "Oh, I see. I didn't—"

"Been down to Washington on a little business," says MacDougal, lowering his voice a notch. He shakes his head. "Hell of a rat race."

"Yes, I suppose so. Well, I—"

"You a friend of mine host's?" asks MacDougal. He gestures toward the far end of the room.

Peale starts to answer.

"Reason I ask is, Pete and I used to be great buddies. We were out in the Islands together." MacDougal lowers his voice another notch. "Matter of fact, that's how I happened to be down in Washington just now. You see, I—this is just between you and me of course—I have certain information I got from the natives out in the Islands that those jokers down in the Pentagon would give their eye teeth for." He nods his head significantly.

"Well, I'm sure they'll be glad to—"

"You see, those boys from the Pentagon just don't know—well, for one thing, you got to be able to handle natives. Now—"

"If you'll excuse me," Peale says, "I'd like to pick myself up another drink. Nice to—"

"Little dry myself. Go with you. Now, as I was saying, you got to be able to handle natives. What I mean is, you've got to understand—well, take the time I figured I'd like to take up copra trading. Lot of money in that. And I've always had a flair for that sort of thing. So I hired me some native sailors and a small outrigger and told them to take me up to this little island in the Fijis that I'd heard about. Natives wouldn't go. Scared silly. Said it was typhoon season. So I decided to go it alone. Matter of fact, I did have quite a storm—but nothing I couldn't handle. Pretty soon I hit this little island, just where I wanted to. Well, this island—you know anything about headhunters?"

"Well, I—"

"Full of headhunters. Full of them. Chop your head off clean as a whistle. Well, I knew it was just a matter of knowing how to handle them. All natives are alike anywhere you go. I'd handled a lot in my day. There's a trick to it, all right. Why, when I was in Africa doing a little job for the government—" MacDougal stops to take in air and drain his glass.

Peale holds up his empty glass. "Look, old man—"

"One time I decided I'd like to do some big game hunting. So I started out from Nairobi one day with a bunch of native bearers. We went deeper and deeper into the jungle. Pretty soon those black boys started getting scared, talked about turning back. So I just told them, 'Now, see here, boys,' I said. 'Let's get something straight—'"

"Bill. We really must go right away." It is Bill Peale's wife. "The Stanleys are waiting out in the car for us."

"All right, dear," Peale says. "Hope you'll excuse me, MacDougal. Nice to have met you." He makes a fast start for the door where his host is standing.

"I know how it is, old man," says MacDougal, going right with him. "The little woman. Got one of my own." He chuckles. "Better come out to the Islands some day. I'll show you the ropes." He winks elaborately and slaps Peale on the back.

You would think that people like MacDougal would be aware that the approval of other people is the last thing their boasting would lead to. Not at all. They have learned to equate their boasting with approval. It signifies approval to them. After all, people do usually listen to them with a certain politeness; and they mistake that politeness for approval. MacDougal feels that Peale thinks he, MacDougal, is quite a guy who has really been around and knows the ropes.

But how did MacDougal get this way? Well, he started early. As a boy he was not outstanding in any way. He had little athletic ability and less academic ability. People paid little attention to him. MacDougal's father did not like this at all. He saw himself as a "live wire" and he desired that the boy develop in his image. But Mac-Dougal, Senior, did not push the boy too hard. He spoke in a kindly way to him of the advantages of not hiding one's light under a bushel—particularly if it were the light of a MacDougal.

The boy, MacDougal, began to heed his father's advice in small ways and found it not unrewarding. Mac-Dougal, Senior, spoke often and at length of his earlier experiences as one of Teddy Roosevelt's Rough Riders and the boy made mention of this in the high-school American history class. The class showed considerable interest and pressed him for details which, fortunately, he was able to obtain without undue difficulty and in some abundance from MacDougal, Senior, together with several cracked photographs. He became, for a time, the center of interest among the boys in his class. It was almost as if he himself had ridden at Teddy Roosevelt's side. Under the stimulus of this approval, he went on to bigger things and soon was recounting with some skill his summer vacation penetrations into the interior of southern New Hampshire.

Starting out in this small way, the boy MacDougal learned that words do at times replace the deed. He has never achieved any position of importance which would rather automatically gain him a measure of approval. But armed with the verbal habits gently passed on to him by MacDougal, Senior, he has suffered no severe frustration of his approval need. And he *was* in the Fijis, having been located there for some time while in the Navy.

Somewhat more successful than the boaster at actually getting approval are the he-man and the glamor girl. These charmers seek the limelight, of course, but much of our society does not disapprove of their doing so because it puts something of a premium on virility and glamour.

In Madison, particularly during the summer, you need not be on the alert to run across people, male and female, who seem to be intent on making an issue of their sex. By offhand estimate, every sixth man is a he-man and every fifth woman is a glamor girl. By day he uncovers his hairy chest on the least excuse and chins himself on the nearest bar. She covers her chest with the least excuse and suns herself in the most obvious places. By night he struts around thrusting out his jaw, and she struts around thrusting out too.

One may glimpse such an individual even at eight-thirty on a morning in late summer when the shadows are still long and dew glistens on the grass of the Boots and Saddle Lodge—Madison's salute to the Old West.

From one of the cabins under the trees a blond young man with a deep tan emerges and slowly walks to the pool. He wears a white terry-cloth robe and has a striped bath towel draped around his neck. He stops at the edge of the pool. He yawns. He shakes off one slipper and, holding the railing, cautiously sticks one toe in the water. He quickly draws it back. He stands there just looking at the water, his robe drawn tightly around him. The breakfast bell rings.

Soon, the blond young man hears the voices of the other guests as they come along the path toward the pool on their way to breakfast. He jumps up and down three times, tosses off the towel and robe, quickly slips over the side of the pool and gasps as he goes down in the water. He climbs out, breathing hard, climbs the narrow steel steps and is poised and ready on the high diving board as the first of the other guests appears from around the bend in the path.

The blond young man expands his chest and raises his arms. The drops of water on his body glisten in the early morning sun. His brown chest looks enormous above the brief white trunks. He takes three measured steps, gives a bold spring, and executes a graceful, though imperfect, swan dive. He surfaces and, appearing to be under the impression that he is alone, makes sure the breakfast procession is stopping to watch. He drifts face down on the water for a moment and then swims the length of the pool three times, executing a racing turn at each end. He swims the fourth lap in a casual, exhibition breast stroke. Then he hoists himself up over the side of the pool in one coordinated movement. He tosses the drops of water from his blond hair, throws his head back and inhales the morning air.

"How's the water?" a feminine voice calls from the other side of the pool.

He wheels around. "Oh. You surprised me." He laughs. "Didn't realize anyone else was around yet. The water's fine."

A small crowd has gathered on the other side of the pool. Many wear heavy sweaters.

"Isn't it awfully cold?" asks a girl in a full-length coat.

"Cold?" the blond young man says. "Well, a little—but that's when it's most refreshing. Nothing like an early morning dip." He picks up his towel and begins rubbing himself with much motion.

"Ooh, I don't see how you do it," squeals the girl. "I'd simply freeze. You must have a fur-lined skin."

The other girls giggle.

"You get used to it," the young man says. "It was a little hard once, but now I don't even feel it."

"Well, better hurry and get dressed," a man calls. "You'll be late for breakfast."

"Be right along," the young man says as he picks up his white robe.

"You'd better watch out, young man," says an elderly woman with a sharp face. "You'll get the rheumatism." She turns and goes along the path toward the dining room. The others follow.

"I'll be there in two shakes," the young man calls. He starts toward his cabin at a fast trot. Once in the cabin, he jumps into bed and tries to get warm.

Like most he-men and glamor girls, this young man does not do anything particularly well, except possibly swim. But he is able to satisfy his approval need quite well by capitalizing on his looks. He was a startlingly handsome boy and learned early in life that exploitation of his face and chest could lead to approval. And, like most successful he-men and glamor girls, he also learned the necessary habit of appearing fairly casual about this business of getting approval. He is always at a pool or on a boat or playing some game or other. He is always in a setting which allows him to pose with some degree of justification. He just always happens to be there. The setting makes his direct bid for approval acceptable. Then, too, our society's culture makes quite a point of approving the physical paragon. The movies, television, and magazines all play up the gains which accrue to the muscle-man and the siren.

Because they have chosen a way for getting approval which is reasonably acceptable to the society's culture, the he-men and glamor girls are more successful than most other types who try to gain approval directly. They are certainly more successful than Susan Howard, whose attention-getting behavior is so obvious. And generally they are more successful than MacDougal, the boastful type, although we would not imply that the latter is other than a he-man in the truest sense of the word.

Chapter 3

END RUNNERS AND LONG-RANGERS

Our society represses the idea of approval as sex is supposed to have been repressed in times gone by. It is considered in poor taste to admit that one wants approval. As a result, some people learn to gain approval by making an end run. They have learned not to buck the iron line of social unacceptability. They have developed a more or less unconscious habit of going around left end.

Mary White is a typical end runner. She and her husband bought a new home in the Glenhaven section of Madison three months ago. They had just moved in when a girl whom Mary had gone to college with telephoned to say she was in town and would like to come out and visit Mary.

Mary opened the door of her new house and there was Higgie (Maria Higginbotham, class of '48) dear old Higgie, just like when they all lived in South Dorm, except a little heavier now and married to a man named Pease.

After the girls had gone through the process of clasping each other noisily and things had settled down somewhat, Higgie said, "Mary, this is the *prettiest* house."

"Oh, it really isn't much," Mary said. "You should see the house up the road."

"Why it certainly is, Mary. It's beautiful. And the view!"

"Well, Joe and I do like it, but—"

"Well, I should think you would. You've decorated it beautifully, Mary."

"It's awfully nice of you to say that, Higgie. But actually, I don't have much of an eye for color. I got most of my ideas from—"

"Mary! You were always the one with the artistic sense in college."

Mary shook her head twice quickly. "No. No, really.

I don't have an eye for color." She led the way into the dining room. "I'm so glad you came when you did. I'd like your advice on curtains for the dining room. I don't have them up yet."

"What a beautiful table, dear," Higgie said.

"Oh, it's just an old thing we picked up and did over." Mary was very busy smoothing out the corner of the rug with her foot. "We didn't do a very good job, actually."

"Why you certainly did," Higgie said.

"Higgie, what do you think I should use for curtains in here?"

There was considerable discussion about curtains. It turned out that what Mary had had in mind was just the thing, Higgie thought.

The girls went back to the living room and Higgie's eye lit on two water colors. They were scenes of the Grand Canal. "My, those water colors add a lot," she said.

"You think I should use blue for the curtains, then?"

"Yes, I do, dear." Higgie was over by one of the water colors. "Who did these, Mary? They're marvelous." She was looking at the signature. "White. Never heard of him. Oh, White! Of course! Mary, you did these! They're beautiful." She stepped back to admire them.

"Oh, I have to do something to keep occupied. They're really not good. They're only copies of a couple of old photographs I had around."

"Why they're wonderful, Mary."

Mary sat down on the sofa. "Oh, they're not much, really," she said. "Now come and sit down, Higgie. Let's not talk about me any longer. I want to hear all about what you've been doing."

This sort of thing works pretty well. Mary is forever getting compliments because she plays herself down so. Her friends would feel uncomfortable if they didn't disagree with her. Mary is not really insincere, because this habit of hers is for the most part unconscious. And not only does it get her immediate approval but people tend to like her because she is anything but conceited. Of course, her self-deprecation gets a little tiresome after a while. But then we all get a little tiresome in one way or another after a while.

As a child Mary was very bright. Naturally the children in school didn't like this because it drew approval away from them. So they disliked Mary. Mary knew what the trouble was but she didn't know what to do about it. Then she happened to overhear a high-school teacher whom she greatly admired say to another teacher, "Oh, it was really nothing. I was just lucky. I really don't deserve it." The teacher speaking had just won the state prize for teacher of the year. The other teacher said, "Why you certainly do! I think it's just marvelous."

Mary thought she would try that approach and see what happened. It worked fine. When she got a high grade on an examination she said she was just lucky and would probably fail next time. The other students warmed to her. "Oh no, you won't, Mary."

"I've just been lucky up till now. There are lots of people smarter than me and I know it."

"No, there aren't, Mary."

"I got a 'C' in science last week."

"That was a fluke."

"No, I just don't understand science. I didn't deserve any more."

Mary made friends and influenced people. That's how these habits get started. Whenever she ran down her own accomplishments, others invariably argued how accomplished she was. They liked her and they approved of her. Her new behavior worked so it gradually became a habitual, unconscious part of her life equipment.

The habitual liar is a second type who tries to gain approval in ways which are indirect to say the least. By the habitual liar, I don't mean the person who lies only when he gets in a tight spot. I mean the fellow who lies in little ways about practically everything—but always in the direction of putting himself in a better light. He can't seem to resist giving a seemingly informed answer to any question although he usually doesn't know what he's talking about. And he distorts the facts about his past experiences—always in the direction of putting himself in a better light. However, he isn't a boaster in the usual sense. He distorts facts in a casual, matter-of-fact, almost self-effacing way which usually allays any suspicion that he is trying to boost his stock.

Scrappy Young is the kind of person I mean. A young fellow in his early twenties, Scrappy is an average enough type in most respects. And he's quite a likable sort, too. As people say, he'd give you the shirt off his back. He might, but if you asked him the time of day there's a fair chance he would mislead you to the extent of a few hours or so.

I remember one time Scrappy and I were walking down Willow Street, one of the secondary business streets in Madison, when two policemen stopped in a patrol car and asked if we had just seen a man running down the street. A restaurant had been robbed. We hadn't seen a man at all; there hadn't been a soul on the street. Scrappy thought for a moment and then he told the policemen he believed he had. Thought he'd seen a man dash around the corner back at the intersection of Bryant and Willow. He couldn't be sure but —well, yes, he *could* be sure. He had seen a man. Definitely. He remembered now. Small weazened-up fellow?

"Could be," one of the policemen said, and wanted to know which way the man had gone.

East, Scrappy believed. Yes, definitely east. The patrol car went in motion with a lurch and screeched around the corner.

Scrappy explained to me how he never missed taking in all that happened—which was true. And there was a lot that didn't happen which he never missed taking in, also.

Then he shook his head and said, "They'll never get him."

"No. I suppose not."

"No," he said. "These boys that pull the little jobs, holding up restaurants, cigar stores, one-arm groceries, that kind of stuff—they know what they're doing. Got it down to a science." Scrappy flipped his cigarette out into the middle of the street as we walked along. "Cops'll never get him."

He was right there.

"Ever do any detective work?" I said.

"No, not much," he said. "Oh, when I was out in L.A. I used to do a little. Used to help the department out once in a while. I studied criminology some once."

"When was that?"

"Oh, when I was in the army. Went to a special school."

"Ever read a book on criminology by a writer named Christie? A. G. Christie?"

"Mmm." Scrappy thought a bit. "Mmm. Seems as though I do remember that. Yes. Yes, I do. General work on criminology, isn't it? Yes. Pretty fair as I remember. But I'll tell you: you don't find any good books on criminology." He shook his head. "No. You've got to look up the articles in the journals. That's the only way."

Now I'm sure the only Christie whom Scrappy ever read is Agatha and I know that he never studied criminology in the service. But Scrappy just can't help rising to the occasion.

As another example, take the time Scrappy and a friend turned a street corner and almost ran into an old gentleman. The old gentleman looked confused, apart from their having almost knocked him down. He had been looking up at the pole with the street names on it.

"Help you out?" Scrappy said to him. Scrappy never passes up an opportunity to do good.

"Looking for the—the Landons," the old gentleman said. "The Landon family."

"Landon. Landon," Scrappy said, trying to place them. "You have the address?" he asked the old gentleman.

Apparently, the old gentleman had had the address on a piece of paper but now he couldn't seem to locate the piece of paper.

"Landon. Landon. Yes, I think I know who you mean. Live down in Black Row, don't they?" Scrappy asked his friend.

"I don't know," Scrappy's friend said.

"Yes, I'm sure they do. Old folks are they?" Scrappy asked the old gentleman. The old gentleman nodded vigorously.

"Yes, that's them all right. I'll tell you how to get there." Scrappy told him how to get there.

"You sure you know them?" Scrappy's friend said. "You don't want to send him all the way down there unless you're sure."

"No. I know who he means," Scrappy said. He told the old man how to get there again. The old man nodded vigorously and started off slowly.

"No," Scrappy said to his friend, "that's one thing I will say. I never direct anyone unless I'm sure."

Well, as it turned out, Scrappy misled the old gentleman, of course. The Landons live out in the Westville section and have lived there for some years. Scrappy just can't resist giving a supposedly informed answer to any question. But he does so in such a way that people seldom realize he is simply trying to boost his own stock—he just happens to know the answer to everything.

Of course, Scrappy will also lie when he gets in a tight spot. When he does that he is trying to avoid disapproval. But in the main he lies in order to put himself in a good light even though he isn't in a particularly bad light. He wants the approval of other people and this is the habit he has developed for trying to get it. Often he does actually get approval, because if people do not know him well they're likely to think he's an exceedingly bright, helpful young fellow.

Scrappy has a job with the new Madison High School. He is assistant caretaker of the grounds. His job is to cut the grass, mark out the chalk lines on the ball field and tennis courts, and generally keep the grounds in order. Now, he does this well enough; but he manages to have quite a lot of time to spare and he has gradually built for himself a role as a sort of assistant athletic director and coach without gym bag, as it were. Actually, he is something of a help to the athletic director. And the latter welcomes his efforts because it doesn't cost the school anything extra. At times, though, the athletic director wonders if he hasn't been misled a little by taking Scrappy's word for things.

One can see in this a strong motivation on Scrappy's part to increase his prestige. He is trying to create for himself a position which verges on that of a member of the high-school faculty. But he can never really succeed because he has had no training for such a position. Scrappy has relatively high goals in general but he does not possess the ability and training to achieve them. So he has developed the habit of lying to try to fill the gap between the prestige he wants and that which he actually gets.

Scrappy's parents made a great point of wanting him to "amount to something." But they never taught him any of the ways for "amounting." They let him do pretty much as he pleased. He was known as something of a tough kid in Madison; hence the name, Scrappy. His father was given to changing a few facts now and then, himself. His father was always saying that he had had to drive over to Greenville or East Madison on a little business after Scrappy had seen his old car parked in the alley next to MacBride's Tavern.

Now we know that not all people who learn to lie do so by imitating their parents. They often learn by trial and error. They try a lie, find it works, that it gets them what they want, and so the habit develops. But Scrappy saw that his father's explanations of his whereabouts while actually at MacBride's Tavern served to circumvent nicely the possibility of his catching hell from Scrappy's mother. So Scrappy thought he would try the same technique in order to boost his stock a bit. He took to telling his parents how well he had done at this or that in school. And they, eager to have him "amount to something," quickly approved of him for his fictionalized accomplishments. He began to make contributions in school which his teachers felt were interesting and original, although his examinations often left something to be desired.

While Scrappy was in the army, his habit of lying blossomed rapidly. There, he found that as long as he was careful to avoid any indication of bragging, he could raise himself to considerable heights in the eyes of his fellow draftees both by referring to past deeds of his imagination and by always having ready seemingly informed answers to knotty questions of the present. But again and again he found that to gain approval in this way he must appear matter-of-fact about the whole thing, never give the impression of trying to be a big operator. He profited by this experience and learned his technique well.

Upon his return to Madison, Scrappy applied to several colleges under the G.I. Bill and was not admitted because of low scores on the entrance examinations. Therefore, he disdained college because he was "too old for it" at twenty-three, and took the job as assistant caretaker of the grounds at Madison High School.

Having little else in the way of approval-gaining techniques at his disposal, lying has become a crutch which Scrappy can not do without. And so now he reaches for a lie the way an alcoholic reaches for a drink.

Apart from people like Scrappy and Mary White, who try to gain short-range, immediate approval by indirect means, there are several other types who try to gain long-range approval by indirect means. Over the years these long-rangers work to gain positions in society which will, once achieved, automatically bring them a large measure of approval.

The "upwardly mobile" individual is one of these long-range types. Upwardly mobile is the term sociologists use to designate those people who are climbing the social ladder, moving up from one social class to another. It is an awkward term but it is preferable to the term social climber, because the latter has such negative connotations. Here, the term upwardly mobile designates those people who, quietly and often unconsciously, are moving or have moved to a higher social class. They are attempting to gain a greater amount of approval from others in the long run and they are going about it in an acceptable way.

John Buckley and his wife Marie are such people. They live in Beauty Hills now and have two teen-age daughters. But when John and his wife were growing up both their families lived in one of the poorest sections of Madison. John's father worked in the Avon Shoe factory. His name was Josef Bukowski. Marie's father drank more than he worked.

John's father was, in his gentle way, almost fanatical about the matter of education. He believed that education was the key to the door of success. He often took John aside and told him of the wonders to which education led. Because he was a kind and gentle man, John believed him and did what he said, which was work hard in school.

John was valedictorian of his class in Madison High School and he was the star of the football team. On graduation day, there was never a more quietly proud man than Josef Bukowski, sitting in the auditorium with his wife and four daughters. John made a fine speech. After they all got back home Josef Bukowski got a little high on wine. It was the happiest day of his life.

John got a scholarship to the university because an old grad named Carter Stillman wanted to see him on the university football team. John played football at the university. He majored in economics, made fairly good grades, and worked on the side. At first he felt uncomfortable among the other boys, most of whom were from well-to-do families. He felt out of place. But he found that if he tried to act as they did, tried to dress as they did, and was not obvious about trying, they accepted him. By his senior year you could hardly tell him from most of the other boys; his clothes seemed to be a little louder than theirs, but that was about the only difference. There was even a little talk of his being nominated for captain of the football team. And John looked forward to graduation when he and Marie, his girl in high school, would be married and he would get a good job.

On graduation day, old Carter Stillman came up while John was still wearing his black academic robe and said, "Come and see me Tuesday at ten o'clock."

John went to Carter Stillman's office at ten o'clock on Tuesday. Carter Stillman said, "You start work for me as a salesman on Monday morning at eight o'clock. From now on your name is Buckley and for God's sake get yourself a different tie." Carter Stillman waved him away. As he got to the door, Carter Stillman called after him, "Get married soon, too, son."

John Bukowski had his name changed to Buckley, put his flowered tie away, bought three ties that were striped a little too brightly and reported for work on Monday morning at eight o'clock. Four months later he and Marie were married. If her father had not died, John would probably have had to give up his job because the old man, drinking as he did, was getting to be a nuisance in Madison.

John's father liked everything fine except the changing of the name. He didn't quite understand that, but if Mr. Stillman said to change it, it was all right. As John told him, Bukowski was not a good name for a salesman; it might be hard for people to remember.

After five years of marriage, John and Marie Buckley had an income of four thousand dollars a year, two children, and a small house among a lot of other small houses in the Westville section of Madison. And Marie had developed the habit of reading everything she could get her hands on about etiquette and home decoration.

Now and then the Buckleys had dinner with some of

John's business associates and their wives. John and Marie wanted to be like these people who seemed so sure of themselves and yet were not high-handed about it. Some of them already lived in Beauty Hills and took it for granted that the Buckleys would move out there soon. The Buckleys began to take it for granted too.

The men with whom John Buckley worked said they didn't give a damn if he had changed his name; hell of a nice guy, wife's okay, too, they said.

A few years later the Buckleys bought one of the smaller houses in Beauty Hills. It was quite a step for them and they were pretty nervous about it. But soon they were asked to join the Whippoorwill Country Club and they began to send the two girls to dancing classes. They became quite happy in Beauty Hills and they still are. But they have been there seven years now. John has done well and is earning eleven thousand a year, and they would like a larger home. They think they might buy in Fairview Manor. As they say, they like their friends in Beauty Hills but a lot of their friends are also over in Fairview Manor now, and they do need a larger home where the girls can bring their friends on week ends after they go off to college. There is also the fact that John and Marie would sort of like to join the Orange Club. Not that there's anything wrong with the Whipporwill Club, although they often say it is getting pretty crowded, but John feels it would be better business if he were in the Orange Club. A few members of the Orange Club have put feelers out once or twice about the matter of his joining. And you more or less have to live in Fairview Manor to join the Orange Club. You don't have to, but everyone does.

On the other hand, they sometimes think they'd be more comfortable staying in Beauty Hills. They're so well accepted there; whenever one makes a move there is always that unsettled period before becoming fully accepted. But, for the girls' sake, they think they should make the move anyway.

John's father, seventy now, is bewildered by what seems to him the magnificence of their present home in Beauty Hills. He is pleased that they live there but he doesn't like to visit them; he likes them to come to his house. John's mother died two years ago and his father lives alone in the old house with pictures of John in football uniform around the parlor. When John and Marie visit him he always wants to hear about the job with Mr. Stillman. And when they leave he always touches John's head with a forefinger and says, "Don't let the head get big, John."

John hasn't let his head get big. Both he and Marie often think that they have come a long way since the day when John made that valedictory speech at highschool graduation. And they often say that it is all because of Carter Stillman. But it is also because of John's father. It was Josef Bukowski who gently planted the seeds of success in John. It was he who taught John that one way to a place of respect in the world—to the general approval of others—is through education. It is not the only way but it is one which will work. It will work if the individual can also learn and take on, in an acceptable manner, the particular behavior patterns of the next higher social class—the ways of speaking, acting, dressing, and everyday living which are used by that class. And the acceptable way for doing this is to do it quietly, as if it were the most natural thing in the world and, above all, not to overdo it.

John learned to do this in college. There he found that if he acted like the boys from more well-to-do families he would be approved of, as long as he did not seem to make a point of doing so. He continued to learn during the first years of his job in Carter Stillman's organization. His way of acquiring the behavior patterns of the people of the upper middle class worked. He passed this experience on to Marie who was anxious to help him move up the social ladder. They both had to be accepted or neither would be, and Marie learned from him.

The Buckleys have gained a position of prestige in the community. John wears conservative ties now and enjoys a large measure of general approval. It is what he and Marie have worked for. The only thing is, they are so in the habit of moving upward on the social ladder that it is difficult for them to stop. But they have reached the point where they should stop. From here on they are not likely to be fully accepted. If they go on now, they are trying for acceptance into Madison's upper class. And you can't move from the lower class to the upper class in one generation—"it just isn't done." They will be happier if they leave that for their daughters, who might make it through marriage.

Another long-ranger, somewhat similar to the upwardly mobile, is the overworker—the fellow who really drives himself to exhaustion to get ahead in his job. Usually he doesn't realize that what he's after is long-range approval, and some short-range approval too. He rationalizes that he's got to really keep at it to insure security for his wife and kids. Actually they'd be secure enough if he just worked as the average person does. What he really wants is the approval that will come when he gets to the top. And while he is getting there, he doesn't mind if he gains a little short-range approval for being such a hard worker. Often the overworker is also upwardly mobile. But he puts much more emphasis on work than on social matters.

Tom Bartlett is an overworker if there ever was one. Tom is forty, heavy around the middle, and vice-president of Madison Foam Rubber Company. He became a vice-president last year. To be a vice-president of Madison Foam Rubber had always been his goal. As a bright young man in the company, fifteen years ago, he reasoned that once he was a vice-president he could relax and do the things he'd always wanted to do. He knew that he would never be president. The president's son was in line for that. A vice-presidency was good enough. Fifteen thousand a year at the least. His family would be secure. He'd be able to send the children to college, do whatever he wanted, and not be burdened with the top responsibility of the presidency.

Tom Bartlett worked fourteen years to be a vice-president. His goal was to make it by the time he was forty years old. He made it with a year to spare. For fourteen years he drove himself during the day and worked at home from eight to twelve practically every evening. Often he was away on business trips on the week ends. It became usual for him to wake up in the morning thinking about office problems. But as Tom has always said, it was the evening work that made the difference. That really gave him the jump on the other men in the office. He was always that much ahead of them. His evening work was always related to future problems, never to current ones. Besides, if he didn't work in the evening, he felt nervous.

Tom Bartlett married Marge Gage five years after going to work for Madison Foam Rubber. He married the right kind of girl, he has always said. Her father was a veterinarian with a wide practice. When Tom proposed he promised her a vice-presidency. She, momentarily thrown a trifle off balance by the nature of his promise, quickly recovered and said she would like that. Tom took a week off and they went to Maine on their honeymoon. Tom got a lot of long-range thinking done on future office problems. He has always said that week had been well worth taking off, apart from the fact that, of course, Marge and he had a honeymoon they would never forget.

When they returned from their honeymoon, Tom worked harder than ever but somehow they managed to find time to have a child. Tom still says what a little trooper Marge was when she was having young Tom. She was so good about it that he didn't lose an hour's work except in the evenings when he went to the hospital. Not that it would have mattered if he had; he wouldn't have felt nervous taking off for a reason like that.

Now, young Tom is nine and in a private school and wants to be an artist. Tom, the father, is confident the boy will outgrow that. Marge plays bridge almost every afternoon and walks the dogs in the mornings and evenings. Tom does not mind her playing bridge and he likes the idea of her walking the two dogs, each with a plaid dog-jacket in cold weather.

The time to talk to Tom is at lunch. That's the time he always relaxes, he says. Pays off in the long run. Clears the brain for the rest of the day if you take a full hour for lunch and forget about business, Tom says. Besides, he can't relax at any other time. Makes him nervous.

After a small lunch he lights a cigar. "Nothing like a good cigar," he says to you. He has twenty minutes of his self-allotted time for lunch left. He sits back a little in his chair. "This is the summer Marge and I planned to take that trip to Europe, you know," he says. "We planned on it, she and I did, for the year after I got the vice-presidency. But, good Lord, I can't get away for a month now, not to mention six weeks.

"Besides, I think I'd go nuts over there," he goes on. "Nothing to do but look at buildings. Don't think I could take it not being at the office." He draws on his cigar. "Marge is pretty upset about it. Never saw her like that before."

He draws on his cigar again. "Can't understand it. She's got a mania on this trip to Europe. The other day she got practically hysterical, said, well—" he leans toward you. "Well, what she said was, she said she'd kill herself if we didn't go. Of course I got her to admit later she didn't mean it. Still and all, it kind of bothered me."

He leans a little closer. "Probably nothing to it but you know old G.W. is getting ready to retire and I have an idea he's not going to trust young G.W. with the presidency. Probably nothing to it, but it's just an idea."

Well, as one can see, Tom Bartlett has become one of those people to whom work is everything. He has built up overwork habits to the point where he can't ever relax. Tom has his eye on the presidency now, but he will continue to overwork even if the president's son does take over. For years overwork has been the means to eventual approval for Tom. And now when he has reached his goal, the means have come to stand for the end, as is often the case with the overworker. Also, Tom has been getting a certain sort of approval all along because of his overwork habits. People say you can't help but admire him the way he has dedicated himself to Foam Rubber.

Without going into Tom's early life in lengthy detail, we can pick out the main lines of influence which caused him to develop this habit of overwork. Tom's parents sowed the seeds of success in him much as John Buckley's father did in John. Tom's parents were a little better off financially than John Buckley's father. But like John's father they had had little education and believed education was the key to success. Work hard, get high grades in school, and you will be a success in life, they believed.

Tom Bartlett did work hard in high school and like John Buckley he got a scholarship to the university. But John Buckley's scholarship was for his athletic as well as his academic ability. Tom Bartlett's was for his academic ability only. Tom had no athletic ability whatsoever. And his personality, unlike John Buckley's, did not attract people at all. He just never seemed to have anything interesting to say; and so people paid little attention to him. He wanted people to like him; he wanted their approval but he did not get it. As early as high school he turned to overwork in the form of overstudy as a compensation. He gained a measure of local recognition because of his resulting academic success.

At the university he continued the habit of overstudy as a means of compensating for his rather colorless personality. He won several academic honors and was highly approved of by the faculty although not particularly by his fellow students. With his record he had no trouble getting the job with Madison Foam Rubber. By that time overwork had come to stand for approval to Tom Bartlett.

At first, the younger men in the company took a dim view of his habit of working so hard. But as they saw that he did not make any obvious attempts to draw the attention of the executives to his industriousness, they came to like him as a sincere, if slightly uninteresting fellow.

In recent years Tom has broadened out a bit and occasionally plays a round of golf on the week end. But out there on the fairways he's always a little uncomfortable because he can't help thinking that he's wasting time that could be better spent on Foam Rubber.

These people, Tom Bartlett, the Buckleys, Scrappy Young, the perpetual liar, and Mary White, the self-deprecator, are all trying to win approval without being obvious about it. They have learned to need approval and, depending on the influence of their environments, they have learned their particular habits for trying to satisfy this need indirectly. Their habits do not work perfectly, of course. Tom Bartlett's overwork causes unhappiness for his wife. The Buckleys will probably be rebuffed if they insist on continuing to climb the social ladder. When Scrappy Young's lying is recognized for what it is, it is not viewed with the highest favor. And even Mary White's self-deprecation sometimes wears a little thin. Nonetheless, if these people did not have any fairly workable habits for satisfying their needs for approval, they would be terribly unhappy people. As it is, each is a reasonably happy, adjusted person.

Chapter 4

CONSTRUCTIVES

WHAT about people whose behavior is particularly constructive—the creative people or the philanthropists or those who are genuinely kind from day to day? Are they motivated by this need for the approval of others? Take Madison's artist, John Burnett. Is his creative art motivated by a need for approval? People think John Burnett is a little queer but not for the usual reasons they think artists queer. He doesn't have long hair, but ten years ago he gave up a good income doing magazine illustrations in order to paint as he wanted. In the main he paints animals. His pictures are unquestionably good, but he doesn't sell many. There doesn't seem to be much market for them and he doesn't have any ability for pushing them. He probably clears two thousand dollars a year at best, and he has a wife and young boy to support.

John Burnett's house stands by itself outside of Madison. Burnett paints in what was designed to be the living room because it has better light than any other room in the house. The family use the small dining room for a living room. The odor of turpentine is in all the rooms of the house, but it is strongest in the room where John Burnett paints.

He steps back from the easel now and squints at the canvas he is working on and then at the dog lying asleep on the floor and then back to the canvas. He pulls his head back, chin in, each time he squints. You could stand in the doorway watching him and he would never know it.

The dog is a red setter which John Burnett has drawn or painted half a dozen times, and now he is painting him again. On the half-finished canvas, you can feel the weight of the sleeping dog against the floor-boards.

John Burnett squints again. Then he walks up to the canvas on the easel, old rag in the left hand, brush in the right, and as the brush touches and goes along the canvas, you can see the curve of the dog's relaxed foreleg come into being before your eyes. There it is, the leg of a sleeping dog where there was only canvas before.

Burnett steps back again and squints, trousers hung low so that the cuffs touch the floorboards. Slowly the dog gets up and walks straight across the room and on out into the hall. Burnett watches the dog go and then stands looking at the canvas. Finally, he cleans his brushes and goes out on the porch. His son, a boy of about ten, is cutting up an old leather jacket with a pair of scissors. He is going to make a pair of moccasins.

"Want to walk up to the rock, son?" John Burnett says.

"Okay."

They go down the porch steps and up a path with high grass curving over it from both sides. The boy is ahead, swinging a stick at the tops of the grass. John Burnett walks along slowly, looking up at the sky.

They come to a slanting, rocky field, go up and across it, in under the trees and, still going up, come out on a wide rock. To the west, the country rolls away into the sunset.

John Burnett stands looking out to the west. The boy goes up on a rise on the rock and walks carefully along a crack in it, intent on keeping his toes right on the crack.

Burnett turns and looks up. A hawk, dark and clear, glides on the wind. Burnett watches him, head back. The hawk glides across the sky and then drops, fast and dark, straight down and out of sight behind a hill.

Burnett stands looking at the spot where the hawk went out of sight. He shakes his head and says aloud, "Beautiful."

Then he sits down on the rock and watches the sunset. The boy watches with him. When the sun is gone, he starts down through the trees and the boy follows him.

Now it doesn't seem logical that a man like John Burnett is motivated to creative work by a learned need for approval. If he is, why didn't he continue to illustrate for magazines? He gave up an income which would necessarily lead to at least a fair degree of approval. The point here is that magazine illustrating actually meant disapproval to him. Money is not the only thing which stands for approval. Burnett felt that magazine illustrating was prostituting his talents. That may be or it may not. But that is the way he felt about it and many of his friends, artists who for one reason or another were not illustrating for magazines, shared his view and disapproved of his doing it.

But leaving aside the fact that illustrating meant disapproval to John Burnett, the central issue is this: is a man like Burnett really motivated to creative work by the need for approval? And if so, how?

Isn't the artist born with an urge to create, a need to express himself? No, actually he is not. He may be born with greater than average perceptive abilities and with a better than average brain, but these will not lead to creative work except under certain environmental conditions. The urge to express himself, to create, is wholly learned under the press of environmental influence.

John Burnett has been drawing and painting since he was four years old. His mother was an impractical woman who could not cook, but she loved nature and she loved art. She herself could not paint but she encouraged her son to draw and paint. She bought him an easel and a painting box and she took him out in the country when he should have been in school and set up his easel for him.

John Burnett's father was a highly practical man and he did not like any such foolishness. He owned a hardware store and he liked the idea of selling good solid hardware. But he knew his wife and he knew she only became depressed and hard to live with when he tried to put the damper on what he called "the art stuff." He felt that the art stuff was easier to take than his wife's bad moods. However, he could not help but show his disapproval of the boy's spending so much time on art. And the more he disapproved, the more he drove the boy away from him and toward the mother and painting.

The mother instilled in her son the idea of making things look alive as they did in nature. She was pleased with him when his work showed progress toward that goal; she acted as if he had struck her when it did not.

John went to art schol when he was seventeen and in a short while learned all there is to be learned in art school. By the time he was nineteen John had his pictures on local exhibition and, while his work did not sell, it was highly praised.

John had to earn a living but working in a hardware store was the last thing he wanted to do. He did not know how to do anything but draw and paint, so he went into magazine illustrating. His work caught on and he did extremely well.

He married and bought a home. One would have thought he would have been quite happy. But he was not. He always felt uncomfortable doing illustration work for the magazines. Somehow, it seemed wrong to him. His mother had died some years ago but he knew that she would have disapproved of it strongly. She had been almost fanatical about the idea that he should make things look alive. And he could not do that in magazine illustrating. He was forced to draw what the particular magazines required; being forced, his work had a superficial quality which was eye-catching but as dead as wallpaper. Then too, the friends he had made who were also artists and who did not do magazine illustrating—either because they had tried and been unsuccessful or because they wanted to paint as they pleased—insisted that with a talent like his it really was a shame to waste it.

As a consequence, Burnett threw over magazine illustrating and now does the kind of painting which has come to mean approval to him. He gets the self-approval which is a reflection of his mother's influence. And he gets the approval of certain of his close friends, both because he is using his talent as they think he should and because they admire the quality of the work itself.

On the other hand, John Burnett's work is not widely recognized and he feels the frustration of that. He will tell you that he believes his work should receive much wider recognition and acclaim than it does. It is the need for all of these three forms of approval—self-approval, the assurances of his friends, and general recognition and acclaim—which drives him on to work of lasting value.

Up the road from John Burnett lives quite a different type of man. His name is Carvel Boynton. He is probably the wealthiest man in Madison; he is certainly the leading philanthropist in Madison.

Boynton has built a hospital for Madison, a public park, and a new library. Recently he added a swimming pool to the public park and even thought to have a half-dozen swans put on the nearby lake. Boynton will not allow any of his gifts to Madison to be named after him.

The Boynton money was made in banking by Carvel Boynton's grandfather, Ezra Boynton. Carvel's father, a vague if good man, managed not to lose much of it and Carvel Boynton has doubled it. Carvel Boynton is a fine man and sincere, though perhaps a little odd. Likes to drink beet juice and usually holds his trousers up with a piece of rope. He's not a show-off—just has a few unusual habits. He enjoys having the townspeople over in the afternoon for a drink. "Beet juice, anyone? Fill your glass?" he calls out. Everyone likes him but many find themselves able to drop over for a drink only infrequently.

In spite of his eccentricities Boynton is a quiet, almost shy man and does not like to have any attention brought to himself. He goes through life doing what he thinks is best for Madison, his wife and daughters, the Boynton money and himself, with his trousers held up by a piece of good rope and a glass or two of beet juice for lunch.

It is obvious that Carvel Boynton does not consciously seek public acclaim by his philanthropic behavior. If he did, he would have his name plastered over half of Madison. Some philanthropists do this, which is all right if they want to. History records the case of a philanthropist who had his name stenciled on the swans he gave his city—philanthropists are always giving a few swans—but the ink was not as indelible as it had been believed to be and the swans looked somewhat unusual until after molting season.

However, Carvel Boynton is not given to that sort of thing. He wants approval but he wants quiet approval. And he gets quiet approval in the passing words and glances of grateful people. These things mean a great deal to him, as they would to any man. It is the need for this feeling of knowing that he is sincerely respected, thought of as a fine man, which motivates Carvel Boynton to philanthropy. In the environment of a conservative family which shunned ostentation he learned that this was the acceptable form of gaining approval.

The need for approval is often the motivating force behind behavior which results in social good. The fact that this is so does not lessen the sincerity and worth of that behavior in the slightest. Some of us feel that deeds of good will cannot be genuine if motivated by a desire for recognition. We feel that way because we have learned to repress the idea of approval as a motivating force; our early environment has been one where it was not considered quite nice to recognize the need for approval. However, good deeds have to be motivated by some need. They do not come about by magic. Rather, they are the most acceptable and finest way of fulfilling our need for approval.

Of course, some philanthropists are motivated by the need to avoid disapproval as well as by the need to gain approval. They feel that they made their money in ways which are, shall we say, slightly devious. Perhaps they are right. At any rate, as a result, they feel vaguely guilty because they have learned to feel that such devious ways mean disapproval. So they assuage their guilt by giving back part of what they have acquired.

Incidentally, Carvel Boynton's idiosyncracies—holding up his trousers with a piece of rope, drinking beet juice, and the like—are motivated by a desire to avoid disapproval and gain approval. Unconsciously he feels that these habits mark him as a man who does not set himself above the common man. And that is just the effect his habits do have on other people; they feel he may be a little odd in some ways but "he certainly doesn't try to set himself above everybody else."

Another man who is also a philanthropist, though a different kind of philanthropist, is Joseph Ryder. He is a mathematics teacher at Madison High School and has been for the past thirty years. He gives away help to his students and a rather bristling brand of kindness—not the help and kindness which a teacher is paid to give his students during school hours but a kind of extra-curricular variety which is not given much space in the high-school teacher's manual.

The following scene has occurred, with minor variations, many times. A boy knocked on the front door of Joseph Ryder's old house and waited. There was no sound inside. The boy knocked again. Then he heard noises inside. Someone was trying to open the front door. The door opened suddenly and there stood Joseph Ryder, his white hair sticking out from his head.

"Come in, boy, come in," he said. Ryder was puffing and he could not get the front door closed. "Damn door, damn door," he said and let it stand ajar.

"Well, come on, boy. Let's go, let's go," he said and started up the stairs. The boy followed him.

They went into a small room furnished with empty shelves along all the walls, a big desk, three chairs with the stuffing coming out, and a large blackboard leaning up against some of the shelves.

Ryder sat down at his desk and put his hands in one pocket after another. He pulled out a pipe, filled it from a can of tobacco on the desk, spilling tobacco over the desk and his knees, went through his pockets again, pulled out a box of matches, and lighted his pipe with the fourth match. "Well, boy, how are you? How are you?" Ryder asked.

"Fine. Fine, thanks, Mr. Ryder," the boy said.

"Let's go, boy. Let's go. No time to waste. Grab the chalk," Ryder said. He tossed his hands around as he talked.

The boy picked up a piece of chalk from a shelf beside the blackboard. Ryder jumped up, pieces of burning tobacco scattering from his pipe. He thumped the boy on the back. "Let's go, boy! Let's go. First problem: circle's got a radius of five inches—come on, boy, get it down on the board! Get it down!" Ryder gave the boy the rest of the problem, thumping him on the back every other sentence.

"Okay, boy. Work it out. Work it out," Ryder said. "That's right. That's right."

Ryder went over to his desk and lighted his pipe, scattering tobacco over the desk and floor.

The boy finished the problem. Ryder kept glancing at the blackboard. "That's good, boy. That's good," Ryder said. "Here's another. Get it down, boy! Get it down."

The boy worked mathematics problems for an hour, going faster and faster, Ryder helping him when he got stuck, thumping him on the back when he shouldn't have gotten stuck.

Then Ryder, breathing hard, sat down in his big chair. "That's enough for today, boy," he said. "You're going good, boy. Want to go to college, don't you, boy? We'll get you there. We'll get you there."

The boy waited.

"All right, boy. That's all for today," Ryder said. "Come back Thursday. I've got work to do. You let yourself out, boy."

The boy went to the door of the room. "Thank you very much, Mr. Ryder," he said.

Ryder hopped over to him and thumped him on the chest. "You're doing good, boy. Doing good. Keep at it." His white hair was sticking out from his head and his eyes were very bright.

The boy went down the stairs and out the front door, leaving it ajar. As the boy walked down the path to the sidewalk, he turned and looked back and up at the house. There was Mr. Ryder inside the window, looking down at him, shaking his head and smiling to himself.

Perhaps Joseph Ryder is not the typical kind person. But he is without question an exceedingly kind and good man. He spends fifteen to twenty hours a week outside of the regular class hours helping students achieve a firm academic foundation. In the past thirty years Ryder has helped a hundred boys and half as many girls get into good colleges. He is well versed in physics and chemistry and he helps the students with those courses as well as with mathematics. The Madison High School is not one of particularly high standing and none but the top student or two in any class would be able to get into a good college unless he had special help.

Kindness is learned just as are practically all forms of human behavior. Kindness is a way of gaining approval which people learn under certain environmental conditions. First, as a child, the individual makes some form of behavior which his society considers kind. He does this either by trial and error or by imitating someone, usually his parents. Then, if the kind behavior is rewarded, the habit of kindness begins to develop. The reward generally takes the form of approval given the child by his parents. If so, the child learns that kindness on his part will lead to approval.

As the individual matures, he may learn to give himself approval for his kind behavior: he knows other people will approve so he anticipates their approval. But this self-approval must be supported by at least occasional approval by others if it is to have any reward value to the individual.

On the other hand, if the individual is not rewarded

for kind behavior he will not learn it as a habit. Suppose a child is born into a family whose members are so frustrated, and consequently aggressive, that they are suspicious of, and disapprove, any display of kindness. If the child does something kind, through trial-and-error behavior or imitation of someone outside the family, he certainly will not be rewarded for it; he may be punished, ridiculed, disapproved. In such an environment he will not learn kindness but, rather, he will learn its opposite.

Such a person as Joseph Ryder has learned the habit of kindness well because his past environment has provided him with many situations which led both to initial occurrences of kind action by him and to reward in the form of approval for that action. Conversely, his environment has seldom frustrated him with disapproval. To put it simply, Ryder's parents were good, kind, sensible people who gave him as a child much affection and who approved of him when he imitated their kindness and disapproved of him when his behavior was unkind.

Ryder has had his share of sadness: his wife died of cancer several years ago, one son was killed in the war. But he goes on with the habits of kindness founded in childhood and built up over the better part of a lifetime. He is reaching out for approval in the most acceptable way known to men—through kindness. And approval comes to him. Practically everyone who knows him thinks that in his own way he is quite wonderful. And he is. Also, he has learned to give himself approval for his actions—approval which is backed up by his knowledge that others think highly of him.

Ryder's behavior helps both others and himself adjust to the world around them. There is little finer human action than that.

PART II

APPROVAL
AND
DISAPPROVAL

Verbal Extremists: Then she said brightly, "Well, I must be off . . ."

Just as they learn the need for approval, most people in our society also learn the need to avoid disapproval. When individuals, as children, fail to do what their parents think they should do, their parents tend to punish them, to frustrate their needs. The parents do this in an effort to train them both to avoid doing things which may lead to physical injury and to avoid acting in ways which the parents consider to be socially unacceptable. At the same time the parents show disapproval of them —reprimand them, scold them, temporarily withdraw affection, and so on. The parents show disapproval for two reasons. One, they are emotionally upset at the prospect of the children's being hurt or falling into socially unacceptable habits. And two, they want to impress upon the children the necessity for avoiding in the future habits which either are likely to lead to injury or are socially unacceptable. Gradually the children learn that disapproval goes with, and stands for, punishment and frustration. Thus they learn the need to avoid disapproval, and this carries on into adult life.

Many of the behavioral habits which people learn are directed toward trying to satisfy at the same time this need both to avoid disapproval and to gain approval. We shall consider some of these habits in the following three chapters. Then we shall go on to habits which are directed solely toward avoiding disapproval.

Chapter 5

VERBAL EXTREMISTS

PEOPLE who talk incessantly are generally trying to avoid disapproval and to gain approval at the same time. They may not do a very good job of it in objective terms. But usually they unconsciously feel and sometimes even consciously think they are doing a good job of it.

Take my good friend, Mrs. Beazley. I ran into her in the Madison Savings Bank the other day. Mrs. Beazley is one of those people who always seems to be there when you go to the bank or the post office or the drugstore.

Mrs. Beazley saw me right away, before I had a chance to go out the other door, and she said, "How nice to see you. How have you been?"

"It's nice to see you—"

"I am so glad," she said. "You are just the person to help me. My son, William, you remember William, of course, has told his father and me that he wishes to be an anthropologist. He is at that stage, you know, only twenty, and we must ease him away from the idea gently. What do anthropologists do, anyway?" She took out a cigarette but hardly paused. "Playing about with old bones. His father wants him to be a doctor or a chemist at least but we must be very gentle with him, he is a very sensitive boy and we must not set up any of those blocks in him. I was thinking that you might be able to suggest how we should handle him."

"Does he do well at chemistry?" I asked.

"The only thing he does well at is anthropology. I remember reading some years ago about a man who contracted a fatal disease digging up old bones, do you remember that? And William's father has not been at all well, he works too hard, much, much too hard, poor dear he flew to California just last week out and back in four days, airplanes are still very dangerous don't you think? I read in the paper just this morning of a crash in Bolivia killing forty-five, or was it forty-six, and there was also something about a crash in Montana or one of those places. Of course the weather has been very bad it is so depressing this time of year I always think it seems as though spring will never come don't you? The winters are not like they were but then so many things have changed I remember when your aunt and I were girls the winters were so much different then we used to skate on the river. Did your aunt ever tell you about the time we all skated to Hampton? I'm sure she has, we all started early in the morning—"

I changed my weight to the other foot and she told me about the time they all skated to Hampton. It took all day—the trip, I mean; she boiled her account of it down to ten minutes. Then she said, "I really must not keep you, I must be off too it has been so nice to see you."

"It's been nice to see you," I said.

"I do so wish William would get this anthropology out of his head what do you think? Do you think we should be firm with him or do you think we should just—I just don't know what to do the young people today seem so unsettled, so very unsettled, but how else can they be? Wars, wars, and more wars, what is it all about? I just don't know. Sometimes I think that if people would just live their lives quietly everything would be all right—" She paused in thought.

Then she said brightly, "Well, I must be off."

"I'm sorry that I haven't been of much help about your son," I said.

"Oh, but you have. I feel much better about it. His father and I will simply explain to him," she said, and she was off.

As Mrs. Beazley went sailing out the door there was a pluck at my elbow. I turned around and there not six inches away was Jack Brown's face. "Quite a talker, isn't she?" he said.

"Yes, she certainly is."

"What was she talking about?" Jack's voice was quiet but seemed to have a note of urgency in it for no good reason at all. His sparse black hair was uncombed as usual.

"Talked about her son," I said. I was at the bank teller's barred window finally.

"Know him myself," Jack said and shook his head. "Queer apple."

"Little wonder."

"Always reminds me of a fellow I used to buddy with in the service. When we were going through France this fellow and I used to—"

"I don't mean to be abrupt, Jack," I said. (This was certainly a bad day for me.) "But I've got to get over to the post office before the mail goes out. Good to see you."

"I'm going that way myself. I'll just go along with you. This fellow, this fellow I used to buddy with in the service, he'd been some sort of anthropologist. Now and then we'd come across some bones as we went through France, lying alongside the road, you know." Jack stopped for breath.

He seemed too close, as always. I led the way out to the street. He was right behind.

"You know what he used to do?" he said.

"What?"

"I say, you know what he used to do?"

"No. What did he used to do?"

"Well, he used to collect these bones. He'd skin any flesh off them, you know. Just slice it off as nice as you please with a special knife he always carried around. Fish knife, it was, as I remember. You know what a fish knife looks like?"

"Yes."

"Well, he used to strip them clean and take them along, as many as he could carry."

I was at a dog trot now but he was right up with me.

"You know what he used to do with them?"

"No. Well, I've got to get this letter registered and get it in the mail," I said as we approached the post office. "Nice to see you, Jack. Drop by the house sometime."

"Thanks, I will."

I went into the post office and up to the Registered Mail window.

There was a slight tug at my sleeve as I passed the letter under the window bars. "You know what he used to do with them?"

I looked around. There he was. Too close.

"Do you know what he used to do with them?"

"Do with what?"

"With the bones."

"No, I don't know what he used to do with the bones."

"He used to wrap them up and leave them with the people at the next farmhouse. Then he'd mark down the exact position of the farmhouse on a map he carried so he could go back and get them after the war."

"Did he?"

"Did he what?"

"Did he go back and get them?" I asked and immediately regretted it.

"Well, it was like this. You see he and I split up at the Rhine and I didn't see him again until the end of the war and—"

I led the way out of the post office and he kept talking behind me as we passed through the revolving door.

"—it was on the way back on the troopship," he went on. "He came up to me on the deck, third day out it was, as I remember, no, maybe it was the fourth, no, it couldn't have been, must have been the third. Well, anyway, he comes up—no, it was the fourth day out—so he comes up—"

"I've got to catch this bus, Jack," I said on the spur of the moment and swung onto it. The bus was crowded. Jack made a stab for it but the doors closed and it pulled away. I could imagine him, standing there still talking.

I hoped I hadn't hurt his feelings but a person can take only so much in one day.

Now, there's a brace of talkers who seem average enough to me, as those of the unzipped lip go. They both have developed this habit of talking incessantly as a way of trying to avoid disapproval and of trying to get approval. Neither one of them was getting much approval from me, I'll admit, and they weren't avoiding my disapproval. But the main point is this: they *thought* they were avoiding disapproval and even felt they were gaining a little approval or were at least pointed in the right direction for it.

These talkers feel that they can cover up their shortcomings by talking. Usually they are people who have not achieved the goals they had hoped to achieve. They feel their failure is disapproved of by others and they try to make up for it by talking. They feel, unconsciously, that their talk draws attention away from their lack of achievement. They also feel that if they talk about what they consider interesting things, other people will necessarily be interested and therefore approve of them as interesting people.

The fact that they don't actually avoid disapproval

and don't actually gain approval is beside the point, because they are not aware of it. They are not aware of it because their listeners don't make them aware of it. In our culture it is considered impolite to be abrupt to people who talk to you no matter how much they talk or how boring they may be. As a rule, we react to the excessive talker as though he were interesting and welcome. And of course, sometimes he is. But generally you have the feeling that he has ensnared you in an invisible verbal net from which you can not escape without resorting to the cutting edge of rudeness. And you are reluctant to do that, of course, because it is disapproved.

Mrs. Beazley and Jack Brown are both people who have not achieved what they had hoped to achieve. They have not gained the status in society which automatically would bring them the approval they need. Mrs. Beazley has always wanted to be one of the first ladies of Madison. But her husband has not been particularly successful in business and she cannot afford to live in Fairview Manor, Madison's top residential section. And she has not been accepted by the Fairview Manor group. She feels that this puts her in a relatively disapproved position and she has developed the habit of talking to try to cover it up. Also she actually feels that her talking gains her positive approval; she feels that the things she says are interesting and stimulating to others.

Jack Brown is still young, about thirty, but he too has not achieved what he had hoped to achieve. He is a clerk in a man's clothing store. I never go in there myself, but they say he is quite a good salesman. However, he has always wanted to be a man of importance. He would like to be a radio or television commentator, something of that nature. But he has no particular abilities, training, or experience for anything out of the ordinary so he tries to fill up the gap by talking. He learned from his parents this need to be someone of importance and, having fallen short of it, he feels the need to avoid disapproval. His parents were always talking about what a smart boy Jack was and how he would make something of himself when he grew up. They overlooked, as parents often do, the fact that he had no outstanding abilities—except for talking. So now he is left with the goal unfulfilled.

Like Mrs. Beazley, Jack feels that his talking leads to approval as well as to avoidance of disapproval. He really believes that other people think, "Now there's a fellow who's really a stimulating conversationalist—like a breath of fresh air."

Another type who has developed a somewhat extreme habit for avoiding disapproval and trying to gain some approval in the bargain is the fellow who seems to think it will cost him at least a moderate sum to say a word or two. Then when he does say something, he says it in such a way that you don't quite know what he's talking about but you think you should. He plays it pretty close to the chest. He enjoys being enigmatic. When, through no fault of your own, you happen to run into one of these fellows after one of the talkers, you have to change gears pretty fast—and I suggest reverse if at all possible.

You run into him at a cocktail party, say. There he is, clutching a glass as if it were about to jump out of his hand.

"How are you, Bill?" you say.

His face looks frozen. He nods. Then he just waits.

"Lot of people here," you say, forced into saying something.

He takes a swallow of his drink and then looks straight ahead. You know him fairly well but say to yourself that enough is enough and start to walk away.

"Reminds one of Eleanor Roosevelt," he says.

"What?" you say, turning back toward him.

"She reminds one of Eleanor Roosevelt."

"Who?"

He nods to the far corner of the room. He means the hostess. You look over at her although you know her well. She has much tooth but little height. "A little," you say.

"Had a cigarette holder a foot long." He laughs abruptly.

You know you shouldn't but you say, "Who?"

"What?" he says.

"Who had a cigarette holder a foot long?"

He looks as if any fool would know that. "Husband."

"Oh. Her husband?"

He nods and takes a drink.

"Funniest damn thing you ever saw," he says. Then he looks straight ahead, frozen again.

"Mmm," you say. "I saw a horse chew betel once."

He looks startled, then frozen.

You walk away. You can be enigmatic, too.

This fellow plays it pretty cool because he is afraid of making a fool of himself. He wants to avoid the possibility of disapproval. As long as he acts as he does, people may think him a little odd but they will not disapprove of him in the usual sense. They will not think him stupid or unsure of himself. Often, they will show signs of admiration: "Bill's an odd apple, but smart as a whip. Comes out with some of the damnedest things. Doesn't give a hoot for anybody, either. Got to admire him in a way."

By just not saying anything he throws people on the defensive. They tend to cast around for something to say. They say it and often it is an obvious or silly statement, because they've felt the need to say something. As soon as they say it, they feel foolish and this fellow Bill doesn't help them any. Either he looks straight ahead or he looks as if they've made a stupid statement, which they have— but because he has forced them into it. And yet they sort of respect him; in a way they would like to be like him. He may be a little queer but he seems in command of the situation.

Now Bill is no wiser and no more sure of himself than anyone else. Actually, he is less sure of himself than most people. It's just that he has developed this habit of appearing enigmatic as a way of avoiding disapproval and of getting some approval in the bargain, and it works pretty well.

Bill was one of those children who are always younger than the other children in school. His parents were what are known as sophisticated people and they pushed him in school. He was fairly bright and they took great pride in explaining to their friends that Bill was two and a half years younger than the other children in his grade.

Being over two years younger than the other children, he was also considerably smaller. He was treated as a baby by the other children. Naturally, he was very unsure of himself. He would try to say things to get approval, and the other children would laugh at him and make fun of his small size. So he learned to say little.

His parents sent him to college at sixteen. He was by no means a genius, but he was quite bright. He had done fairly well in high school and could do college work satisfactorily. But at sixteen he looked about fourteen, at the most, both in face and physique.

The older boys, men of the world at eighteen, some of whom shaved as often as twice a week, always asked each other, "What's that?" when they saw him. On the defensive, he would look straight ahead and say nothing. He learned that if he kept quiet, even when asked a question, it gave him a chance to size up the situation.

Then, at a freshman dinner, the other boys at his table were talking about what a crochety old geezer the Dean was. They started calling on each other for speeches. Suddenly they called on Bill. They hauled him to his feet. He was stricken but he was not going to let them know it. He looked frozen. There was silence. He had had two glasses of beer and he said, "He can go to hell."

"Who? Who?"

"The Dean," he said and sat down.

He hardly knew he said it. But the other students cheered him, slapped him on the back, and drank up. They went on to other speeches but this was the beginning of Bill's habit of saying unexpected things. The habit, together with the habit of generally saying little and looking frozen, worked very well. He avoided disapproval and gained some approval in a backhanded way. He branched out and began saying obscure things—not too often though. By the time he graduated from college his present approach was well congealed.

Bill did graduate work in chemistry and is now a research chemist for the Madison Foam Rubber Company. As is the case with many individuals, he unconsciously gravitated toward an occupation which suits his personality; he deals with things rather than with people, fortunately. One can hardly imagine him a rousing success as a salesman.

Chapter 6

SELF-IMPRESSED

POMPOUS PEOPLE, social snobs, and pseudo-intellectuals are generally individuals who have been either hurt by disapproval or threatened by it. They have their backs to the wall a bit; their habits, which make them seem overly impressed with themselves, are the only ways they have been able to learn for dealing with the situation. At the same time they have not been too severely hurt nor too seriously threatened by disapproval and so they are also concerned with attempting to gain a measure of approval while they avoid disapproval.

There are some in Madison who feel, and perhaps with some justification, that Colonel J. Doubleday Lombard, U.S.A., Ret'd., Superintendent of the Madison Military Academy for young gentlemen, leans at least slightly toward the pompous side. Colonel J. Doubleday Lombard, U.S.A., Ret'd., came to Madison Military Academy two years ago. The Board of Governors had been looking for a recently retired army officer to replace the aging superintendent, and Colonel J. Doubleday Lombard seemed to fill the bill perfectly. He had had a career distinguished for his assistance to distinguished generals. He was offered the job. He hesitated for what he felt to be a respectable period of time, long enough to give the impression that he was weighing other offers, and then accepted in view of the fact that "training leaders for this great country of ours comes before personal gain in my book."

Colonel Lombard took command of the Madison Military Academy with a keen awareness of his responsibility as the leader of future leaders of men. He gave first priority to a new motto for the school which he had painted in big red letters on a large blackboard and hung by two thin wires in the middle of the large main hall of the administration building. The sign read "Distinguished and Forceful Leaders through Distinguished and Forceful Leadership!"

Colonel Lombard recognized as his first task at Madison Military the necessity to "banish the confusion rampant here, and set this house in order." He began this task by calling a meeting of the military and teaching staffs.

The members of the staffs gathered in the auditorium. The speaker's rostrum was decorated with red, white, and blue bunting. But Colonel Lombard was not in evidence. Then a bugle call faltered through the air and Colonel J. Doubleday Lombard, short and heavy, marched down the aisle in full dress. His dark blue full-dress cape was flung back over his shoulders, exposing the red lining. Colonel Lombard was flanked by three short cadets, also in full dress. He mounted the steps and encountered no difficulty until he gained the stage. There he caught his toe in the aging carpet; he recovered nicely. He surveyed the auditorium slowly. He pursed his lips. He whispered to one of his aides. The aide took a deep breath and called loudly, "Attention!"

The members of the staffs looked around and then gradually rose to their feet.

Colonel Lombard surveyed the scene. "Gentlemen—" he paused. "Be seated."

Colonel Lombard looked to the left, he looked to the right, he looked to the center. "Gentlemen, I come here as a leader of men. My primary mission is to set this house in order. Every well-organized unit, no matter what its nature—and there is no such thing as a unit without organization, gentlemen—every well-organized unit must have a leader whose authority is undisputed. Gentlemen, I am the leader here. Therefore I must have that undisputed authority in order to expedite my mission."

Colonel Lombard looked right, left, and center. Then he cleared his throat. "Gentlemen, every one of you has a duty to perform. And if you neglect to carry through that duty—" he looked at each man: some shifted the position of their legs—"then you have not done your duty."

Colonel Lombard waited. Then he whispered to an aide. The aide called, "Attention!"

Followed by his three short aides, Colonel J. Doubleday Lombard strode down the steps and up the aisle, shoulders well back, eyes straight ahead, chins up. He stopped at the door. He whispered to one of his aides. The aide turned and called out, "Dismissed!"

Since that day two years ago, Colonel Lombard has taken many steps to set the Madison Military house in order. All the fire hydrants have been painted a khaki color. All streets on the campus have been made one-way streets. Bulletin boards have increased in number from sixteen to eighty-four. Striped sentry boxes dot the campus at strategic points where before there stretched only unbroken land. A low-numbered license plate has been obtained for Colonel Lombard's staff car. And those cadets who master-minded the "Down with General J. Popinjay Blowhard" movement have been apprehended and drummed from the corps.

Nor has Colonel Lombard ignored the importance of smooth public relations. Each month he contributes an article on "Leadership is Everybody's Business" to the *Madison Times-Herald*.

Now the colonel is a good enough sort when he lets his hair down. Of course being bald around all but the edges handicaps him a little in this department. At any rate, as a young officer he was not particularly pompous. But he was, we must report, something of a bumbler. That is, he seemed to be forever saying and doing small things which made him seem a little foolish—not stupid things, just awkward, bumbling things. For example, he would frequently go through a doorway or around a corner and run into and almost knock down a senior officer. This sort of thing provided much grist for the humorous mills of his fellow junior officers if not for those of the senior officers whom he so encountered. On one occasion he sent sprawling an aging lieutenant colonel of cavalry. The old warrior regained his feet and immediately attacked, face red and mustache awry. "Lieutenant, explain your action," he bellowed at the then Lieutenant Lombard.

There was silence.

"Speak, man. Speak," bellowed the lieutenant colonel of cavalry.

"Sir, it—it happens all the time," said Lieutenant Lombard.

As J. Doubleday Lombard slowly climbed the officers' ladder toward generalship he gradually developed pompous, blustering habits which to some extent obviated the possibility of his bumbling so badly. He walked with a slower, more deliberate stride. His face took on the aspect of indignation. He took to clearing his throat considerably before speaking, thus giving himself opportunity to marshal his thoughts. These habits were rewarding to him in that they did tend to keep him from bumbling into situations which led to disapproval. Then too he was no longer a junior officer, and the officers and men under him necessarily showed the required outward respect. This he mistook for approval of his ways.

As a young man, J. Doubleday Lombard wanted to be a general more than he wanted anything else in the world. And until his late forties J. Doubleday Lombard looked forward to that day with confidence and serenity. In a locked box he kept the two silver stars his fiancée—who later broke the engagement and married a musician—had given him the day he was commissioned. But as the years went on and J. Doubleday Lombard faced his fifties, he began to realize that it was highly unlikely he would ever become a general. He simply wasn't getting there fast enough. Retirement age would arrive and he would be only a colonel. He began compensating ahead of time. His pompous habits increased. His voice grew deeper and more authoritative. His walk became a strut. As his belly grew out his shoulders went back. As his hair grew thinner his expression grew sterner and more indignant. It was as if he were unconsciously trying to say, "Take note, I am a man of consequence, even if I am not a general."

Retirement came and J. Doubleday Lombard's goal of being a general was made irrevocably unattainable. The job of superintendent of the Madison Military Academy was offered him and Colonel Lombard seized upon it. Now he is a big frog in a small pond. To him, that is preferable to being a smaller frog in the large pond of retirement. But he is still not a general. So he lives the part of a general—as he sees the part of a general—commanding two hundred and eighty-nine active, if not seasoned, troops.

Like the colonel, the pompous are usually large frogs in small ponds who have failed to achieve the golden goals they once cherished. And they are unconsciously doing their best to make up for it. Their behavior continues because it is somewhat rewarding. They have created for themselves an illusion of approval and a curtain against disapproval. Since they are big frogs in small ponds, the other frogs have to give the impression of approving of them. The other frogs cannot afford to indicate to them that their behavior is really leading to disapproval rather than approval.

The social snob is a second self-impressed type who, like the pompous, is attempting both to avoid disapproval and to gain approval. One such was in residence at 44 Fox Lane, Fairview Manor, on the evening of October 2.

"I believe that includes everyone," Marguerite Standish said. She put down the list and her little gold pencil. "I shall send the invitations out tomorrow morning. Will you please see to the wines and liqueurs, Malcolm?"

"Okay, I'll call up the store tomorrow," Marguerite Standish's husband said. "Marge, I really wish you'd invite Eleanor and Bill. After all, they—"

"Malcolm, we have been all over that. It is simply out of the question."

"But Christ, she's my sister. And Bill is really a nice fellow when—"

"Malcolm, please. Please do not say 'Christ.'" Marguerite Standish closed her eyes and shook her head slowly. "I have explained to you about Eleanor and Bill a dozen times. If you have no sense about those things, I do. We can have them for dinner sometime when no one else is going to be here."

"But Eleanor seldom gets a chance to see any of the people she used to know and—"

"Eleanor," said Marguerite Standish, "should have thought of that before she married Bill. I cannot invite him here when the Worthingtons and the Holdens and people like that are going to be here. What would they think? Be reasonable, Malcolm."

"They'd think he was a nice fellow. Everyone does."

"Oh, he's nice enough, I suppose. That is not the point.

He's just not our sort. And may I remind you that he is completely self-made—a self-made real estate agent." She touched the right side of her graying hair with extended fingers.

"But he's perfectly—"

"Yes, yes, I know," Marguerite Standish said, waving her hand slowly. "He talks and dresses quite correctly, if overconsciously. But it is not the same. After all, it is background that counts. You cannot deny that blood will always tell."

"Well, just in case you don't know it, I've taken Bill to the club with me several times and—"

"Malcolm, you've taken Bill to the Orange Club?"

"—and the boys all like him, think he's a great fellow. Herb Worthington wants to put him up for membership."

"Well, I must say I certainly don't understand Herbert Worthington. I thought at least he—"

"And I'll tell you something else. I'll bet you that the Worthingtons and Holdens think it's damned queer we don't have Eleanor and Bill here. We always have your sister and that half-wit she married. If there's anyone who is really a social dud, it's that boy."

"My sister did not marry beneath her," Marguerite Standish said. "Carrington Carruthers has breeding. He is from a fine old Maryland family. There is no problem—"

"Fine old Maryland jackass."

"—there is no problem about inviting my sister. Mother, thank goodness, brought us up to have the proper regard for such matters. Apparently your mother—"

Phyllis, the Standish's sixteen-year-old daughter, rushed in from the hall. "Mother, Jim Dugan wants me to go to the movies with him this evening. Is it all right? It's a swell picture with Bunny de Grant."

"Phyllis, please do not say 'swell.' I do not know who Bunny de Grant is, and I do wish you would not run around in those frightful clothes. They're horrible. Take them off."

"But Mother, everyone wears blue jeans."

"Whom do you mean by everyone, may I ask?"

"Why—all the girls. Ethel and Janie and, you know—all the kids."

"Phyllis, you are not everyone," Marguerite Standish said. "Now what was it you wished to do?"

"Jim Dugan wants to take me to the movies."

"And who is Jim Dugan? Not that boy who lives in the old Clark house?"

"That's him," said Phyllis. "He's lots of fun. May I go?"

"Let her go, Marge," Malcolm Standish said.

"I shall not forbid you to go, Phyllis," Marguerite Standish said. "But I wish you would not go. The Dugans are very middle class."

"Mother, Jim Dugan is the most popular boy in school," Phyllis said. "All the girls are crazy to go with him."

"Then let him take all the girls to the movies. Phyllis, why can't you associate with boys like Peter Worthington?"

"Fats Worthington? Mother! He's a perfect drip! I'd sooner be dead."

Marguerite Standish looked from her daughter to her husband, shook her head and said, "No one in this family but I, I'm afraid, has any regard for the things which really matter."

Marguerite Standish's snobbery is a defense against her own insecurity. She does not feel secure in her own social position. The Standishes have moved into Fairview Manor only recently. The people there like them well enough, but Marguerite feels that perhaps they are not fully accepted. Malcolm Standish is a vice-president in the bank, but it is a small bank. Neither he nor Marguerite has any inherited money to speak of. They came from average middle-class families, not from families who have always been in Madison's upper class. In one corner of her mind Marguerite realizes this although she denies it with the rest of her mind. She constantly tries to convince herself and others that she and Malcolm are "blue-blooded."

Marguerite is afraid of disapproval from those who do feel secure in the top levels of Madison society. And she wants their approval. So she uses this habit of looking down on others to boost her own security. If others are lower socially, then she feels higher. This helps her to assume that those in the top levels of Madison society will approve rather than disapprove of her. Also, she is afraid to associate with, or to have her family associate with, people who are in Madison's middle or lower classes. She is afraid she will become identified with those classes and consequently be disapproved of by the upper-class people.

Marguerite Standish's sort of snobbery is generally passed on from parents to children. The parents feel insecure socially, are striving to be accepted by a higher social class, and they teach their children this defensive snobbishness. The children at this point have learned the normal needs for gaining approval and for avoiding disapproval. But their parents, being overly concerned with the problem of social acceptance, have taught them only snobbishness as a way of trying to satisfy those needs. The parents have drilled into them that emphasis on their "breeding," which may actually be quite average, and on association with the "right people," stands for approval and avoidance of disapproval.

When Marguerite Standish was a child, her mother was much as Marguerite is now, only less accepted by Madison's upper class. Marguerite's father was a gentleman bookkeeper. Her mother feared the "contamination by commoners," as she put it, of her daughter. She was constantly telling Marguerite that she was better than other children because of her breeding. Her breeding was of an average enough sort but, of course, Marguerite had no way of knowing that. However, the main point is that Marguerite got approval from the very fact of her mother's telling her she was better than other people. And she was disapproved of by her mother whenever she associated with anyone who was not high on the social ladder. Thus it is little wonder that Marguerite has developed habits of snobbishness as ways of attempting to gain approval and avoid disapproval.

The pseudo-intellectual is another type of snob who seeks to both avoid disapproval and gain approval by his behavior. You will not find many pseudo-intellectuals in Madison but if, in season, you journey to the nearby university, you may chance upon an occasional Madison expatriate, maybe even two or three.

There in a room with newly leaded windows, two young men sit limply in armchairs. One young man is thin and one young man is fat.

The thin one says, "What did you think of Alabama's latest?"

And the fat one answers, "It was a terrible disappointment, really."

"Yes."

"I think I shall return to Eliot."

"No."

"Yes, really."

"Come."

"What else?"

"Maugham, perhaps," says the thin one, laughing softly.

"One could hardly return to Maugham, having never been—oh, let's not talk rot."

"Maugham sells well," chuckling softly.

"Cheap perfume sells well, my dear fellow," answers the fat one.

"I have a wonderful story about Maugham."

"Please."

"Really. It happened just the other day. Daughter of friends of the family was asked by her instructor to evaluate Maugham's contributions. Dear girl was at a loss, naturally. Finally she said, 'I simply would not know where to begin. The old gentleman seems to have forgotten to put the symbols in.' "

The fat young man considers and then says, "Odd way of expressing it."

"Priceless, *n'est-ce pas?*"

"I must run down and get the new issue of *The Tiny Review*," says the fat one. "See you anon."

"Must you?"

"It's all one has these days."

"But it's so tiny."

"Dear boy. Size is the most vulgar aspect of our culture today," says the fat one.

"I must agree."

"I must go," the fat one says and slowly rises. "See you anon."

"Au revoir," breathes the thin one.

Young men like these have become pseudo-intellectuals because they have failed to gain approval and to avoid disapproval by more conventional means. Their intellectual posing is a defensive measure against disapproval. Since they are usually members of a group of pseudo-intellectuals, they gain approval from each other. They also enjoy feeling superior to those who are not aware of the very latest intellectual styles.

Pseudo-intellectuals such as these two young men usually come from early home environments where they are over-protected and not taught the aggressive yet acceptable habits necessary if one is to compete in a modern society like ours. Often such an environment is one where the mother strongly dominates the home or where the father is totally absent. The mother is always fearful the children will be hurt and does not allow them to participate in any of the everyday rough-and-tumble situations which prepare children for a competitive world.

As a result, such boys are afraid of athletics and are often outstandingly awkward in adolescent social situations. They gain little approval from other adolescents, are in fact disapproved of, looked on as pantywaists. Because of the mother's overpowering influence, the boys often develop effeminate mannerisms through imitation of her. (This does not necessarily mean that they are also developing homosexual tendencies, which is quite a different thing.)

If young men like these go to college, they inevitably find there a certain group of older students who, like themselves, are not athletically inclined, who feel uncomfortable at beer parties, but who have cultivated to a high degree the pursuit of new intellectual fashions (or for that matter, of certain old fashions.) This group of students lives somewhat apart from the other students and its members approve each other, disapprove those outside the group, and avoid the disapproval of the latter by remaining within their own little group. They are glad to accept new "members" because this strengthens their group. The only real requirement for admission to the group is a willingness to appear intensely interested in what is currently the intellectual fashion. So, young men such as the thin young man and the fat young man quite unconsciously gravitate toward pseudo-intellectualism and thereby find a way to gain approval and to avoid disapproval.

The pseudo-intellectual, the social snob, and the pompous are often hard to take because they seem to be, and in fact are, disapproving of others in order to raise themselves in their own eyes. But remember: they are people who have been hurt and this is their unconscious way of trying to adjust.

Chapter 7

OVERDOERS

THERE is a final group of people who direct their behavior toward both avoiding disapproval and gaining approval. This group is composed of those who overdo a good thing. Like the self-impressed, they are sometimes a little hard to take. Some overdoers carry the banners of morality into the cloying regions of self-righteousness. Some would reform the alcoholic by denying the man in the street his glass of beer. Others would make an unending fetish of honesty. Still others would not stop at doing you a good turn but would go on to the point of killing you with kindness.

On the one hand these people feel guilty. They feel they have done or thought things which are severely disapproved. And they are trying to alleviate these guilt feelings by over-compensating, going all out in the other direction. Actually they may have done or thought little which is disapproved, but they *feel* they have. These feelings are usually a result of an overly severe upbringing and of oversocialization. On the other hand, these people want a measure of approval and they say in effect that, by heaven, they are going to get it no matter how far they have to push a good thing.

However, I would not advise you to go up on the porch of 15 Vine Street, Madison, and tell that to Mrs. Hannah Comstock. She, the lady of the house, has just finished her daily chores. The laundry is out on the line, the beds are made, the dusting's done, the sink is scrubbed. In her afternoon dress of gray cotton with white collar and cuffs, her graying hair arranged in a tight bun on the back of her head, Mrs. Comstock sits down in her porch rocker to read.

She picks up a copy of a women's magazine, turns the pages, and soon puts it down. The magazines these days are getting worse and worse, she says to herself. Full of pictures of women half undressed and young folk sitting around on beaches and always picnicking and wasting their time instead of working and earning their way in the world like they ought to be doing. The young people these days are lazy and useless enough without magazines putting more ideas in their heads. No wonder the world is in the state it is. When she was a girl, people worked and didn't spend their time on foolishness and fixing themselves up and running around the way this younger generation does. And glad she is of it, too. Those of her day were good hard-working people, not lazy loafers.

Look at that young couple that moved in across the street—how could they ever amount to a hill of beans, Mrs. Comstock wonders. It's shameful the way people like that are allowed to move in where decent folk are trying to lead a decent life. All summer, nothing but picnics in the back yard in the evenings and drinking, sometimes until way into the night when people should be in bed and asleep. And the two of them, the young woman practically undressed, sitting in the sun on Sundays instead of going to church and mowing the lawn. They're a disgrace to the neighborhood. Thank goodness she and Walt aren't like that and can look people in the eye.

All that people like that young couple seem to think of is how to get out of their share of the world's work so as to have more time to spend on loafing and sinning. Washing machines and electric mixers and all that nonsense just makes flibbertigibbets out of them. Of course, how else would you expect young ones to turn out these days with all this talk about child psychology—as if there was any psychology in a child. When she was a girl it was "don't spare the rod and you won't spoil the child" and that's the way it should be. Every child should have his hide tanned now and then, it's the only way to make something of him. Many's the belting she had when she was a girl and it made her an honest, decent woman who was not afraid to face her Maker on Judgment Day.

Worst of it is, it's the idlers like those people across the street that get all the butter and cream these days. Spend the first quarter of their lives loafing, learning blasphemy and the like. And then start out earning more than someone who's toed the mark and learned useful work, like Walt who's spent his life in the mill. Honest toil counts for nothing these days. Well, the devil takes care of his own, they say. And the devil will take care of the idlers and the sinners down there where the fires burn mighty hot!

They'll find out on Judgment Day what listening to the devil leads to. And the Lord won't need any psychologist to tell him who's good and who's bad. He'll know who's lazy and who's sinful and who's not, and those that are will be mighty sorry when they see us that aren't, walking down the Golden Streets. And it will serve them right, too.

Mrs. Comstock goes on like this to herself and to others much of the waking hours of every day. However, she is not really a crank. She's a good-hearted soul, as they say. It's just that she cannot help feeling that it's terrible the way most people sin and loaf. When she is not thinking about this to herself, she is generally talking about it to her friends or listening to them talk about it.

Mrs. Comstock thinks as she does because she feels guilty. She has never actually done anything which is considered immoral. But she feels that she has. She was brought up according to impossibly strict standards of morality. She was oversocialized in the extreme. She has necessarily fallen a little short of those standards in her daily life, as anyone would. As a result, she has guilt feelings. Or to put it another way, she feels she has done things which lead to disapproval. She feels this unconsciously, is not aware of it in her conscious thoughts, but it motivates her self-righteous behavior nonetheless. By seeing others as immoral, she sees herself as more moral. Thus she tends to avoid the threat of disapproval for immoral acts which she unconsciously and mistakenly feels she has committed.

Furthermore, there is the fact that Mrs. Comstock would, in a way, like to have a bit of fun herself. But the conscience aspect of what Freud would have called her superego—her learned need to avoid what she feels her society considers morally wrong and therefore disapproves—won't let her. So she disapproves of those who do have fun and sees for herself eventual approval in afterlife as a reward for her present abstinence. She also gains considerable immediate approval as a result of her contributions to her friends' discussions of the proposition that immorality is rampant in the world.

With Mrs. Comstock's earlier environmental experience it is little wonder she now carries the banner of self-righteousness. Her parents pursued morality with the determination of a pair of bulldogs. They fiercely trained their daughter to take her moral place in an immoral world. She gained approval for nothing short of saintly behavior. They taught her that evil threatened at every small turn along the road of life. Take the time her mother found her playing in the old barn behind the house with George Small, the boy across the street. It was an hour before her fifth birthday party. The barn was dirty, she had already been dressed for the party, and so she had taken off her dress to keep it clean. Her mother hit her, sent George home bewildered, and dragged her to her room, screaming all the while, "Don't ever, ever do that again!" Her mother locked her in her room and was ill for two days. There was no birthday party and when her father came home from his day's plumbing, he whipped her grimly.

Mrs. Comstock has completely forgotten this incident. She has also forgotten the recurring dream she used to have when she was in high school—that a slim boy with curling hair would sweep her onto his horse and carry her to strange, castle-topped hills, and make love to her. Because of the disapproval which she learned to associate with such innocent pieces of behavior as these, because of her inevitable failure in later life to live up to the fierce code her parents taught her, and because she learned from them that approval came only to the morally perfect, in short, because of oversocialization by her parents, Mrs. Comstock has over-reacted in the direction of self-righteousness as a way of avoiding feelings of disapproval and gaining some approval.

Mrs. Comstock is in many ways a broadminded woman compared to those fortunately rare individuals whom one might call professional reformers. These individuals fix upon some social practice or other and pursue its reform with a zeal which, if directed toward other ends, might well relieve a good deal of misery in the world. One such reformer is a female relative of mine, distant in genealogy if not in space.

Recently this middle-aged lady blocked my way and pressed her perpetual question with usual vigor. "Young man, can you say one good thing for alcohol?" she asked me.

"A drink, now and then, is relaxing," I said.

"Young man. Evil is never relaxing. Sleep is relaxing." She looked like a youngish Grandma Moses with a hangover.

"But sleeping is often impractical—before dinner, for example."

She fixed her eyes upon me. "Young man. Do you not realize that half the world's ills are due to alcohol? Hitler was an alcoholic. Roosevelt drank. Over half the crimes of this country, including murder by automobile, are committed by persons under the influence of drink."

"I don't think—"

"Negroes are notorious drinkers. More Negroes are arrested for drunkenness than any other one thing."

"That is true for whites, also."

"Very likely it is. Young man. There is only one way to save the country. And that is to pour every drop of alcohol on the ground and prohibit the manufacture, importation, and sale of the vile liquid."

"But consider the question of why people drink, madam."

"Don't be silly, young man. Because they can get it." She lowered her head and looked over the top of her glasses with narrowed eyes and said very slowly: "Because they can get it."

"Yes, but—"

"There are no buts. If alcohol were not available people would not drink," she said. And armed with this unassailable bit of logic she went off to do further battle.

Now this good lady is rather like Mrs. Comstock only more so. She had a strict, oversocialized upbringing. Thus she has had guilt feelings throughout much of her life. She has never done anything which our society would term morally wrong, but in the course of normal living her behavior has often not come up to the impossibly high standards taught her in her childhood. Thus she has often felt that her actions were disapproved.

She has learned to compensate for and dispel these feelings of disapproval by going overboard in the direction of reform. In so doing she gains considerable approval as well. After all, right is partially on her side; excessive drinking is considered a sign of personal maladjustment. Then, too, there are many others who, also desirous of reforming the tippler, approve her actions enthusiastically.

Why does she fix on drinking as her target for reform? Why not gambling, prostitution, or politics? Because drinking, more than any other social practice, has come to stand for the threat of disapproval in her eyes. Her father's brother was the bane of her parents' existence when she was a child. He drank excessively— he was the blackest sheep of the family—and her parents went to great lengths to avoid him. She learned that drinking spelled disapproval in the extreme. Then when she was a young woman during the prohibition era she had a few drinks herself with a college boy who self-admittedly knew his way around; she found them disconcertingly pleasant at the time of intake though severely depressing in the disapproving light of retrospect. She crusades against alcohol rather than against some other practice because she thereby provides a defense against her own desire to tipple at least moderately, that desire signifying disapproval to her because of early learning. Since her conscience won't "let" her drink and since she would like to drink, she salves her conscience by zealous crusading.

Generally, then, reformers are people who have been oversocialized in childhood and who are trying to avoid feelings of disapproval and to gain approval by crusading against the practice which to them most signifies the threat of disapproval.

Another type who overdoes it a bit is the scrupulously honest fellow. He is not trying to reform the world. He is content to simply carry his own honesty to a point whch makes even Abe Lincoln seem a little on the shady side.

Nine out of ten people don't worry too much if they overlook some very minor sum on their income tax statement. Most of us would not cheat the government grossly but a slight error in our favor does not seem too bad. When we get back a dime too much change in a store and do not realize it until we arrive home, most of us neither go back to the store nor return the dime by mail. And I don't know about others, but when I get back too much change and realize it at the time, I call it to the clerk's attention but always with a little pang of regret in my heart.

Allen Marsh, "Honest Al Marsh—Insurance of All Kinds," as it says on his card, is different. As he will often tell you, he is annually afraid he has overlooked some minor sum which should have been declared on his income tax. When he gives the clerk back the dime too much which he received in change, he gives a little lecture on the joys of being honest right along with it.

I remember driving over to East Madison with Allen about a year ago. On the way he stopped for gas. A little later, as we approached East Madison, Allen slowed down and pulled over to the side of the road.

"You know, I have a feeling that young fellow back at the gas station made a mistake in change," Allen said. He took out his coin purse and his wallet with the rubber bands around it, removed the rubber bands expertly, and took count. He rubbed his chin. Sure enough, the boy had undercharged him.

He swung the car around and we went back fast. At the garage the boy was sitting on a bench listening to the ball-game on the radio. Allen got out of the car and went over to the boy. "Say, son, I believe you shortchanged yourself a while back when I stopped for gas." He had the coin purse out and the rubber bands off the wallet.

The boy looked dazed.

Allen took count again.

"Yes, just as I thought," he said. "The gas was two dollars and ten cents, as I remember. I had twenty dollars—two ten-dollar bills—and just a couple of cents change when I stopped for gas. Yes, I'm sure of that because I remember thinking I didn't have any change to speak of. And now I have seventeen dollars in bills and over a dollar in change. You see, I couldn't have that much unless you short-changed yourself. You see that, don't you, son?"

The boy nodded uncertainly.

"Yessir, son, you short-changed yourself at least ten cents, maybe a few cents more. I don't know how many pennies I had originally. Tell you what," he said to the boy, "we'll call it fifteen cents—couldn't have been more than that."

He handed the boy fifteen cents. The boy took it. "You want to be careful, son," Allen said. "Some people wouldn't have realized you short-changed yourself." He put the rubber bands back on his wallet, carefully put it and the coin purse in his pockets, and came back to the car whistling.

The boy watched him get into the car.

Allen headed the car for East Madison once again. "You know," he said, "people are getting so careless these days that plain old-fashioned honesty is getting to be more than a full-time job."

We will all agree that honesty is an admirable and necessary thing. But Allen Marsh carries it to quite an extreme, one must admit. He thrives on the sort of thing that happened at the gas station. One good incident like that a day would keep him on top of the world indefinitely.

Basically, Allen Marsh is much like both the self-righteous Mrs. Comstock and the good lady who would banish tippling for all time. Because Allen was taught impossibly high standards of honesty as a child, he feels as an adult that he must be on guard at all times against the eventuality of his own dishonesty. So he goes to extremes in the other direction—that of honesty with a vengeance. And the habit works nicely for him because not only does he avoid a feeling of insecurity over the possibility of disapproval but he gains a feeling of approval as well.

Allen makes quite a point of recounting to others, in a matter-of-fact way of course, his numerous successful experiences in the field of nth degree honesty. He is saying, in effect, I really am very honest, don't you think? He feels that your answer is yes and that you approve of him. And of course your answer is, in effect, yes, and you do approve of him. What else can you do? He is right, almost too right. You can't quarrel with him. But I sometimes think that once in a while he convinces himself he has been undercharged just so he can win another round with honesty.

Last but not least in the overdoer group we have the do-gooder, the person who just does you so much good it hurts. I ran into one of these people not so long ago on a trip across the state from Madison to Tavistock. I seemed to have gotten on the wrong road. So I pulled off to the side and stopped the car at one end of a small town.

As I was checking the road map I heard a voice call out, "Help you, mister?" I looked up and there, coming fast across the lawn from a large, old house, was a large lady, one Mrs. Dingle as I later learned.

"Hot, ain't it?" she said. "Where you going, mister?"

"I'm trying to get to Tavistock. I seem to have taken the wrong road back there somewhere."

"Tavistock? You really done it, mister. This here's Danville. You're heading for Allentown. Where you coming from, mister?"

"From Madison. Well, I'll just go back to—"

"Just like I thought. You took the wrong turning back at Boone Corners. Lots of them does. Road on the left goes to Tavistock. You forked right."

"Well, thank you," I said. "I'll just turn around and go back—"

"Oh, you don't want to turn round and go all that ways back. There's a short cut over to the Tavistock road. I'll just put you on that. You'll be there in jig time. Now, up this here road about a mile, maybe a mile and a quarter, you come on to a dirt road forking left. It don't look so good but never you mind that. You just fork left there and you go on about two mile, maybe three, then—let's see—it gets a mite tricky but—"

"Well, thanks," I said. "But it's only ten miles or so back to Boone Corners. I'll just go on back there."

"No, no," she said, getting a firmer grip on the side of the car. "This here's much easier once I show you. Let's see, now. You fork off on the old Bailey road for two mile or so, then—you got a map, mister?"

"Yes. But look, I—"

"No trouble at all, mister. Give it here."

I gave it there.

She adjusted her glasses. Finally we found where we were on the map.

She studied the map. The sun was awfully hot. Finally she shook her head. "Map you got there don't tell you nothing, mister. Better one in the house. I'll fetch it. Won't be a minute." And she went off fast across the lawn toward the house, my map in her hand. As she mounted the porch steps she called back to me, "You come up on the porch, mister. Cooler." The screen door banged behind her.

I went up on the porch and sat down. It was cooler.

She didn't come back. Finally the screen door pushed open. It was a dog coming out of the house. Then the woman came thumping out, breathing hard, face red. "Couldn't find that new map we been keeping in the desk. Jim must of took it. No matter. Found this one here up in the store room."

She unfolded the map and adjusted her glasses.

I waited.

She brought the map over close to me. "Here's where you be now, mister. Here's the road you're on. Now, you just go up it about a mile and you come to the dirt road forking left—let's see—I guess it ain't on the map. Wait. I'll get a pencil and—"

"Oh, that's all right. Never mind. I can remember."

"No trouble at all." She went in the house again. This time she came back pretty quick. She had a pencil and a kitchen knife. She got it sharpened and then the point broke off and she sharpened it again.

"Now, mister, you just hold this map up against the side of the house and I'll draw in the cutoff for you."

I held the map up against the side of the house and she started in with the pencil.

"Afternoon," someone said.

I looked around and there was a man in overalls.

The woman looked over her shoulder. "My husband," she said to me, and then to him, "Ed, come over here a minute."

"What is it, Amy?" her husband said. "I've got to get up to the mill right smart."

"Ed, just you put on the map here how the cutoff to Tavistock goes. This gentleman's took the wrong turning back at Boone Corners."

"Ain't no cutover to Tavistock no more, Amy. You know that."

"What you mean, Ed, ain't no cutover to Tavistock

no more? I'm talking about the road goes up around Art Miller's place—"

"Washed out last spring, Amy. Ain't been fixed. Ain't going to be."

"Well, I never," she said.

"Best way to get to Tavistock, you go back to Boone Corners," the man said to me.

"Well, Ed, I just don't believe it," the woman said. Then she said to me, "You just wait a minute, mister. I'll call up Em Miller and see if that road ain't open." She went into the house fast.

"Got to get up to the mill," the man said, and he left.

I could hear the woman inside talking to Em Miller. "We don't get rain soon, everything'll be plumb baked," she was saying.

After four or five minutes she came back out on the porch. "Land sakes, it's hot, ain't it?" she said.

"Yes, it is. Well, thank you anyway—"

"Tell you what you do, mister. You go back to Boone Corners and you fork left. No—let's see—you'd be going back so you fork sharp right, that's it. That's got it. That's better than taking the cutover. Em says it might be passable but ain't too good. Fellow went over it two weeks ago, Em says, but she don't think he made it. Might of, but she don't think so. You best go back to Boone Corners."

"Okay. I will. Thanks very much. Very kind of you." I went down the porch steps and headed for the car.

"Get you something cool to drink," the woman called after me and banged the screen door behind her.

I got in the car—it was like a furnace—and started the engine and turned the car around.

The woman came heading across the front lawn fast, a big glass in her hand .

"Here you be, mister. This'll cool you," she said.

It was a glass of grape juice. I drank it and it was cold, but when I was a boy I had an aunt who was always pouring grape juice down me.

"That's very nice of you. Thanks again," I said.

"Nothing. Nothing at all," the woman said. "What are we for, if it ain't to help each other, I always say."

Then she let go of the car and I got away.

Sure we're here to help each other. But there comes

a time, it seems to me, when you reach a point of no return. Be that as it may, this woman, whom I later learned was Mrs. Dingle, certainly means well. No question about that. But why does she mean *so* well? Couldn't she mean just a little less well?

Of course Mrs. Dingle is not a particularly rare bird. There are a considerable number of people much like her, especially in small communities. They learn as children that it is disapproved to fail to *always* volunteer a helping hand. And they learn that they gain approval from the other people in the community when they do lend a helping hand. This is the stuff of which communities are made, and far be it from me to disapprove of it. Here the important point is that mutual aid in the community hinges on both the learned need to avoid either disapproval or the threat of it and the learned need for approval.

The more extreme do-gooders, like Mrs. Dingle, have learned not only this habit of always volunteering a helping hand. As children, they have also been oversocialized—learned a stronger than average need to avoid disapproval in general. In the course of their everyday adult lives this need, being particularly strong, is necessarily frustrated now and then; situations which lead to disapproval are bound to occur occasionally. As a consequence, the oversocialized do-gooders feel vaguely guilty. To dispel this guilt they unconsciously reach for the main habit they have learned for avoiding disapproval—trying to help others—and they throw it into the breach constantly.

By resorting to the habit, they have a feeling that they are gaining approval as well—and, of course, they are. Even in such cases as that of Mrs. Dingle, you don't really disapprove; you just want to escape. Having escaped, you then reflect on Mrs. Dingle as a good-hearted, well-meaning soul—you approve of her, everything considered. You do this because you have learned that to think otherwise is disapproved, even if the do-gooder is pretty hard to take.

When the do-gooders' attempts to help others miscarry and do more harm than good, the do-gooders sometimes become aware of the fact. If so, they feel disapproved. Then, they try to right the situation by doing more good; they attempt to counteract the disapproval. Since they are overly anxious to right the situation their further attempts often miscarry also. The snowball then gets rolling and cuts a mean gash down the field of social relationships.

PART III

DISAPPROVAL

Shy:
They had taught him
never to fight back ...

MANY PEOPLE develop defensive habits—extreme shyness is an example—which are directed toward avoiding disapproval only, and not toward gaining approval also. Their need to avoid disapproval has been severely frustrated in particular types of situations in the past. When those situations reoccur or threaten to reoccur, they immediately resort to their defensive, disapproval-avoiding habits. Of course, in other types of situations where they have not previously experienced disapproval, these same people will employ approval-gaining habits. A person may resort to shyness for avoiding any situation which involves people other than his closest friends, yet on the job he may employ highly efficient work habits —for the purpose of gaining approval. But when threatened or confronted with situations which have brought them disapproval in the past, these people are so busy avoiding potential or actual disapproval that they do not have time to concern themselves with approval.

Chapter 8

SIDELINERS

ONE GROUP of people who often employ habits directed solely toward avoiding disapproval is made up of those who stay on the sidelines of life. By withdrawing from the field of action they minimize the possibility of encountering disapproval. Mr. Henry Potter of 192 Highland Avenue, Madison, fits into this group nicely. He is as shy a man as you are likely to meet in or out of Madison.

Mr. Potter is a bookbinder and a very good one, too. He is Madison's best, in fact. He was so even before the other one died last year. Mr. Potter was once heard to say, "I like to bind books." He is thin, bony and angular. Although he looks sensitive, he does not look timid or shy—certainly not mousy.

Mr. Potter and his wife live in a pretty little house, formerly a gatekeeper's house, on Highland Avenue where once the finest homes were located. If you meet the Potters when they are out for a stroll, Mr. Potter raises his hat, whispers, "How do you do?" and moves back one step.

From there on Mrs. Potter does the talking. She does not talk excessively and she is not domineering. She simply does the talking for both Mr. Potter and herself.

"And how are the children?" she asks you.

While you are answering, Mr. Potter whispers quickly in Mrs. Potter's ear.

"Mr. Potter was wondering if your boy's tonsilitis has cleared up nicely," Mrs. Potter says matter-of-factly. She calls her husband Mr. Potter both when speaking of him and when speaking to him. Presumably he calls her Mrs. Potter, but there is no way of knowing.

You answer that the boy is fine now and Mr. Potter smiles to show that he is glad all is well and then he quickly looks away.

"Mr. Potter and I are planning a trip to the Carolinas this spring," Mrs. Potter says. Mr. Potter stands with hands clasped together in front of him, looking down to one side.

"That is very nice," you say. "The flowers will be beautiful."

Mr. Potter makes a little sound as if he were laughing. He turns his head quickly toward Mrs. Potter, bends down and whispers in her ear.

Mrs. Potter nods and says, "Mr. Potter was thinking about the time—oh, it must have been thirty years ago —it was on our honeymoon, wasn't it, Mr. Potter?"

Mr. Potter smiles, nods, reddens and looks away.

Mrs. Potter goes on, "We had gone to the Carolinas to see the flowers in the spring but there had been some sort of unusual condition that year and what do you think? The bugs had gotten into every one of them."

Mr. Potter puts his fingers to his mouth and can hardly keep from laughing. His eyes twinkle above his fingertips. Then he quickly composes himself.

When you and the Potters part, Mr. Potter raises his hat and whispers, "Good-by."

Mr. Potter is a trifle extreme, it is true. Basically, however, he is like most shy people, only more so. He does have a certain, elfish sense of humor which is not apparent in most shy people; but then, it is not apparent in Mr. Potter unless he knows you quite well. As one would surmise, Mr. Potter has been, like all shy people, severely hurt by disapproval in the form of ridicule in the past. Now, he feels he must avoid such disapproval at all costs. His extreme habit of shyness, of never entering into the give and take of a social situation except through Mrs. Potter, enables him to do so quite well. Other people may mildly disapprove of his shyness, but they seldom display any external indication of it because they generally perceive that he is extraordinarily sensitive.

Mr. Potter's parents were reserved middle-class people. His father was surveyor for the city of Madison for many years. Both of his parents trained him to do things in just the accepted way. They instilled in him the idea that it was wrong to aggress against other people in any way—no matter what the other people did. They taught him to turn the other cheek. They oversocialized him, trained him to follow the most acceptable rules of society at all costs.

This oversocialization as a child is fairly typical of the shy person. It prevents him from taking aggressive action against other people if he is later severely hurt by criticism and ridicule. When the oversocialized person is severely hurt, he feels that withdrawal is the only acceptable action he can take; he feels that fighting back would only lead to more disapproval.

Usually the ridicule to which shy people have been subjected in earlier life has been due to some personal inadequacy. Take Mr. Potter. As a child he was ugly in the extreme. His head was large and his body scrawny and ungainly. He looked like a caricature of the ugly duckling if ever a child did. The children in school plagued him unmercifully. The offspring of the more "refined" families called him Chicken Potter. The other kids referred to him in more original and less endearing terms.

But Mr. Potter's parents had taught him never to fight back. They had taught him to turn the other cheek. When the other children plagued him, he turned and ran. If he kept away from them, he was all right. Also, he learned that when he couldn't run, it was best if he just kept quiet. People didn't notice him so much. And if they did, they didn't bother him for long. There was not much fun in it for them if he just kept quiet.

So Mr. Potter learned the habit of shyness and withdrawal as a way of avoiding disapproval. The habit became firmly fixed because it was rewarding, because it worked. It kept him from being ridiculed. It satisfied fairly well his need to avoid disapproval and so became a mainstay of his personality.

As a young man, Mr. Potter took a job as an apprentice bookbinder because it was the one job available at the time which required little dealings with other people. Fortunately, the future Mrs. Potter was a bookbinder too and of some experience. She was kind and gentle with Mr. Potter and when she asked him to marry her, he did not say no.

Oh, there are times of course when Mr. Potter would like to be an assertive fellow, a man of action, a devil-may-care type. As well as having a strong need to avoid disapproval, he has a need for the kind of approval those types sometimes enjoy. But the desire for that approval is nothing compared to the anxiety he would feel if he took even the first step away from shyness; it is nothing compared to how he would fell if he ever left himself wide open to the possibility of severe criticism and disapproval.

The recluse is a second type who has learned to avoid disapproval by retiring to the sidelines of life. He has, in fact, retired beyond the sidelines; he has left the scene quite completely. Old Man Largo, as he is known, is the only true recluse I can think of in Madison. Old Man Largo lives outside of town, up on a hill overlooking the old South Turnpike. His house is a gray rundown affair with the glass missing in some of the windows. I missed him both times he came into town last year for supplies. But I had heard quite a bit about him and was curious to talk to him. So I went out to see him. It was awfully still around the old house up on the hill. Nothing moved. Down on the Turnpike the small cars went along slowly and silently.

Suddenly Old Man Largo was standing there by a corner of the house, long, thin arms hanging.

"Hello," I said. "Mr. Largo, I hope you'll excuse my intruding—"

"No," he said and then waited, not moving, his eyes narowed at me.

"My grandfather used to know you when you lived over in Bradford. His name was John Hunter."

"He was a bastard."

"That may be, but—"

"He was a bastard if I ever knew one." Old Man Largo laughed loudly. Finally he settled down. He was still standing by a corner of the house. "I will go one step further," he said. "He was a son of a bitch."

"That's what he always said about you."

Old Man Largo roared again with laughter. When he had settled down again, he pointed his beard toward an old packing box and said, "Sit down."

He looked at me closely and then said, "Did he say he was my friend?"

"He said he knew you."

"I wouldn't call him a friend but he was about the only man in Bradford worth speaking to."

"Why do you say that?"

"Why do I say that? Because I God-damned well feel like saying it."

"That sounds reasonable."

He studied me again. Then he laughed. "By Jesus. You must be his grandson."

"I am. But I only told you I was so that I could get you to talk to me."

"Why?"

"I want to know why you stay up here by yourself."

"Why?"

"I thought I might write a piece about you for the local paper. You're a curiosity."

"You're a meddler," he said. He was still standing by the corner of the building, outlined against the sky.

"How long have you lived here by yourself?" I asked him.

Old Man Largo looked disgusted. He knew I must know the answer to that without asking him. Everyone knew he'd lived there thirty years or more.

"I would think a man would miss children if nothing else," I said.

He laughed loudly again and then said, "They're worst of all."

"What do you do here by yourself?"

"What I damned please."

"What do you do?"

"Think."

"What about?"

"Listen, son," Largo said. "I have work to do."

"I can see you're pretty busy," I said and smiled as I looked around at the weeds. He roared and I went on. "But give me a few minutes of your time anyway. Why do you prefer to live out here by yourself?"

He walked over to me, long legs and arms working like a spider's. He put his face down near mine. His teeth were brownish yellow and so were his beard and mustache, particularly around the mouth. "Penance," he said. Then he fairly blew himself apart with laughter. His eyes watered. Juices trickled down his beard.

"For whom?"

He had recovered. "That is a good question," he answered.

He straightened up and looked for a moment like a thin, old-time schoolteacher who had been lost in the woods for a few weeks. He had one forefinger extended. "For those who try to make themselves feel better by conniving and cutting each other's throats. I do penance for them and get some measure of peace in the bargain." He cocked his head so his beard stuck out and added, "A working solution to a most difficult problem."

He walked away from me and back toward the house where I had first seen him standing. He turned back toward me. "Kindly don't come again," he said and then he laughed.

"Are you happy?" I said. It was a foolish question, but I wanted to see his reaction.

He stopped laughing and looked straight at me. "Is any man?" he said and then he turned and went out of sight around the corner of the house, his arms and legs going like a spider's.

Largo's early years are, as they say, shrouded in mystery. My grandfather knew him slightly when they both lived in the town of Bradford, quite some distance from Madison. Largo was nineteen or twenty then. His parents were dead. He was considered the town oddity. He worked only off and on, as a house painter's assistant. He was given to going without shoes, and his hair was always long and shaggy. He spent a good deal of time reading in the town library. When he wasn't there, he was generally walking in or around the town, his feet bare and his hair streaming. The town's older citizens watched him from behind curtains with smiling mouths and shaking heads. The younger gentry laughed openly and called after him, "Where to today, sport?"

Largo had no friends. There were only the townspeople either watching or plaguing him.

The last day he was seen in Bradford he was pushing an old cart filled with blankets and pots along the main road out of town. He pushed the cart to calls of "Expedition to Alaska, sport?" on out of town. He came eventually to the old abandoned house above Madison and settled there.

From this one can see that Largo had never learned the accepted methods for getting approval. Apparently he had a weak need for approval and a strong need to avoid disapproval. A person with a strong need for approval will never go into seclusion, because the need is too severely frustrated then. On the other hand Largo must have had a strong need to avoid disapproval or the jibes of the town wits would not have had such a marked effect on him.

But Largo's parents, whoever they were, must have oversocialized him in one respect at least—that of not aggressing against others. Otherwise, when the town wits plagued him he would have lashed out at them. As it was, being oversocialized with respect to aggression and without anyone to turn to, he fled society once and for all.

Although it might not at first glance seem logical, extremely lazy people fall within this category of sideliners. They, like the shy and the recluse, are also trying to avoid disapproval by removing themselves from the mainstream of life. Take the case of one Dudley Jenkins. Some of the self-admittedly finest people in Madison say that Dudley Jenkins—commonly known as Dud Jenkins—is the laziest boy in town. The laziest human in town for that matter.

Dud is a bit on the hefty side. Won't do a thing but eat and not too much of that. Doesn't need to eat very much to keep his weight up though, as he never does anything that burns up food quickly.

Dud quit school the day he reached sixteen—the legal age for quitting. His parents didn't like it since Dud had been doing fairly well in school. He had passed his sophomore year with little trouble, but the classrooms for the junior year were on the second story and that was just too much for him. And what could his parents do?

Dud got a job after that working in Schultz's Grocery Store, but he always kind of petered out around eleven in the morning. As a result, he got the sack. Now about all he does is watch the sky. He likes to do that —providing he's pointed in the right direction. About the only exercise he gets is turning into the shade. He strained himself recently while turning into the shade, however, and hasn't been the same since, he says. He may give that up soon.

Dud is a rather nice-looking boy and he comes from

a nice family. He never gets into mischief—too much trouble for him to try. People like him but naturally they're a bit concerned for him.

It often seems as though extremely lazy people are just plain ornery or as though they just won't take the trouble to do anything. But if you look beneath the surface you will always find that they are afraid of disappproval, that they are terribly insecure in social situations. Their laziness is really a withdrawal to the sidelines of life, a defensive habit to avoid disapproval. True, they sometimes incur criticism because of their laziness. But they would rather have that specific kind of disapproval than risk the possibility of various forms of more extreme disapproval were they to enter energetically into social situations. Besides, the criticism of their laziness is often of a light, bantering sort as in Dud Jenkins' case.

Dud Jenkins is intensely afraid of making a fool of himself. There is considerable justification for his being so. In his grammar school years, before he developed his habits of laziness, he involuntarily made a fool of himself much of the time. He was always tongue-tied when the teacher called on him. Actually he knew his lessons but when called upon, he was too nervous to collect his thoughts. One time when he rose to try to answer the teacher's question, his knickers slipped to his knees. His parents always bought clothes "good and big" for him and the top button had come loose. But the other children and the teacher did not make allowances for that. The teacher made him spend an hour in the coat closet ("A big boy like you, not even able to keep his pants up."). The boys in the class attempted to pull his pants down each day during the following weeks. Dud became the class goat.

Why was he so inept? For two reasons: first, because his parents put such extreme pressure on him to "be a model boy" and, in effect, avoid disapproval, that he was always so anxious he inevitably bumbled; and second, because his parents failed, on the other hand, to teach him specific ways of acting which would have enabled him to avoid making a fool of himself. They were so busy telling him to be a model boy that they failed to tell him that he should always wear a belt to keep his pants up.

Dud learned by trial and error that the one way he could improve his predicament was by simply doing nothing. Apparent laziness was the only thing he could hit upon for at least partially reducing the disapproval which befell him and so he took to it wholeheartedly. Like shy Mr. Potter and like Old Man Largo, Dud is trying, in the best way he has been able to learn, to protect from frustration his need to avoid disapproval.

Chapter 9

POOR AVOIDERS

MANY HABITS which people use in attempting to avoid disapproval are much less effective, everything considered, than those of the recluse, the shy person, and the lazy one. The habit of worrying is probably the most common example of an ineffective habit for trying to avoid disapproval. Everyone worries now and then. But some people have involuntarily developed the habit to the point where they spend the greater part of their waking hours worrying.

Out in the Westville section of Madison where small houses stand row on row close together, each with a television aerial, there lives a champion worrier, one Helen Parks. Helen Parks is thirty-seven years old and used to be pretty. Now she is very thin and there is a drawn, tight look about her face. She looks frightened all the time.

There is nothing in Helen Parks' life which, from an objective point of view, should cause her any particular worry. There is no illness in the family, no great shortage of money, no serious problem of adjustment between her husband and herself. Her friends in Westville say they cannot for the life of them see what she has to worry about. She and her husband Bob have a pretty little house and two fine children. Bob is doing pretty well in the insurance business. They may soon even be able to move to Beauty Hills on the other side of town if all goes well. Bob has a piece of land all picked out.

But these things do not stop Helen Parks from worrying. When she awakens in the morning, something to worry about invariably pops into her consciousness: Bob's eyes, for instance. They've been bothering him for several weeks. Maybe, as he says, he just needs new glasses. But there are so many serious things that can happen to one's eyes. Just the other day she read about a man who complained of headaches one day and was stone blind the next week. Suppose Bob went blind like that? He'd want to kill himself. He'd lose his job. What would they do? The children would starve.

Then when Helen looks up into the mirror after brushing her teeth in the morning she worries about getting old. She looks almost fifty already, she thinks to herself. Bob will probably want to leave her soon. She can't blame him the way she looks. She must talk to him about that. Find out if he plans to leave her. Certainly she couldn't blame him if he did. But what would she do? What about the children?

When Helen Parks puts the wash out on the clearest day of the year she worries that it will rain. When she has friends in she is continually worried that they are not comfortable, that they would like something or other that she has not offered them. Wouldn't they like to sit in this chair instead of that one? Maybe they would rather have had a cocktail instead of tea—when they are already drinking the tea. Is the tea hot enough? No, it can't be. She'll make some more. When the friends leave they are worn out. Helen is worn out, too. She worries that perhaps she didn't give them a chance to relax. This is the one time when her worrying has some basis in reality.

Helen and Bob talked over the possibility of the move to Beauty Hills the other evening. Helen was worried about the children. They wouldn't have any friends there. Then, too, the main highway is only a block away from the lot Bob has picked out. How could she ever be sure the children wouldn't ride their bicycles on the highway? And with the number of accidents there are these days they might both be killed. On the other hand, maybe it would be best to move. They would be in the other high school district there. Bob, Junior, might not be on the football team then. And that would certainly be for the best. If he stays on the football team here, he is sure to be maimed. No matter which way you turn these days, there is danger of some sort.

What Helen Parks is really concerned about in all her worrying is the possibility of the disapproval of other people. Each situation she worries about is one which she consciously or unconsciously feels may lead to disapproval. If she neglects to offer her guests something, if she doesn't make them comfortable enough, will they think she's a poor hostess? If her husband went blind and lost his job and they became poor, what would people think of them then? If her children are maimed riding bicycles on the highway or playing football, will people say she was not a good mother, that she did not take the proper care of them? If her husband *did* go blind, if her children *were* maimed, she would, of course, be more concerned about their welfare than about what people would say. But these things have not actually happened and there is very little possibility of their happening. In her worries Helen Parks is more concerned about disapproval than these possibilities in themselves, although she does not consciously realize this.

Helen Parks takes a devil-may-care view of life compared to her mother. There was nothing about which that lady did not worry. She worried that Helen would get some terrible disease in school "with all those germ-filled children." She protected her child against all manner of imaginary evils. "It is better to be safe than sorry," she always said. When Helen was ten years old, she worried that Helen would end up an old maid.

One of Helen's mother's constant worries was that either the Canadians or the Mexicans would invade the United States. She always predicted invasion within a year. With this good lady, it was not a question of whether or not the U.S. would be invaded but rather of which group would do the invading—the Canadians or the Mexicans. She hoped it would be the Mexicans. "They are dirtier but they are lazier," she always said. "At least they won't *do* as much after they do take over the country. . . ."

Leaving the matter of invasion aside, Helen's mother made her feel that it was wrong not to worry and that she should feel guilty for being happy. Whenever Helen was happy, her mother took her to task severely for being "heedless" and for failing to be on the alert for danger and disaster. In effect her mother approved of worry, and she approved of Helen when Helen worried and disapproved of her when she did not. As a consequence Helen learned to worry.

Worrying is directed toward attempting to satisfy the need to avoid disapproval; but it is an abortive habit and fails to lead to any but the slightest satisfaction of the need. About the only rewarding aspects of the habit are that it keeps the individual on the lookout for possibilities of disapproval and that it reduces his learned guilt feelings about being happy.

The major result of worry is, of course, a negative one. It produces anxiety in the individual; anxiety leads to fatigue and to chemical changes in the body which make the person particularly vulnerable to disease. But the individual has not been able to learn any other habits for dealing with the problem of avoiding disapproval, so the habit of worrying goes on.

Extreme indecisiveness is a second inadequate habit which a few individuals learn as a way of trying to avoid disapproval. One of those few indviduals is John Bolo, a bright young garage mechanic at the Madison Tip-Top Service Garage. John cannot make up his mind about anything. He is a pleasant fellow, not at all stupid, but he cannot make a decision about even the simplest things. John can fix an automobile engine because he understands engines, he can find the trouble, and there is only one thing to do—fix it. But if the boss asks him to park a car in the big garage so that it is out of the way, John is lost.

"Where would you like it?" John asks pleasantly.

"Just get it out of the way, John," the boss says, and starts toward the office.

"Over there in the corner?"

"Yeah. That's good."

"The rear end might stick out a little."

"It'll be okay."

"Maybe I'd better put it down there on the other side of the Caddie."

"Okay."

"No, maybe I better not. Might be in Nick's way. He's going to work on the Caddie."

"Put it in the corner."

"I'm afraid it might stick out a bit."

"For Christ's sake. Just park the damned thing!"

"Yes, sir. How about over there?" John says, pointing to a third possible spot.

The boss says, "Jesus Christ," gets in the car, guns the engine, jumps the car ahead and into the corner, slams on the brakes, gets out, and walks away.

John studies the parked car for a moment, says aloud to no one in particular, "Fits in nice," and goes back to work.

There is a running joke in the garage; it concerns which sandwich John should eat. He brings his lunch, as do most of the mechanics. He always brings two sandwiches, a big piece of cake, a piece of fruit, and a thermos of milk. He likes to save one of the two sandwiches and a little of the milk for a snack in the middle of the afternoon. He doesn't have any trouble with the milk but the two sandwiches are usually made of different things and he has considerable difficulty deciding which to eat and which to save. Invariably he asks the advice of his fellow mechanics. It's just an automatic habit with him to ask such things.

"Which should I eat now, the sliced ham or the egg salad?" John may ask.

"Eat the ham," one mechanic says.

"The egg looks good," another says.

"Save 'em both," a third says.

"I'll eat the ham," John declares.

"Do that, John."

"No, maybe I better save the ham. It might keep better."

"Eat 'em both."

"Maybe I better."

"Eat half of each."

"That's just what I'll do," John says. And he does.

Even in the cases of such simple matters as where to park a car or which sandwich to eat, John can't make up his mind because of a pervading, though unconscious, desire to avoid disapproval. He has never had the opportunity to learn to make decisions of any kind, and those he has made have generally led to disapproval. So he has learned equivocation, indecisiveness, as a way of trying to forestall disapproval.

John's parents were forty years old when he was born. They were set in their ways and they were exceedingly strict with him. But their strictness was inconsistent. One time they would punish him rather severely for a given piece of behavior and the next time they would not punish him at all for it. At some later time, they were liable to punish him for exactly the opposite behavior. They believed in the fact, rather than the logic, of strictness and punishment. As a result John grew up never knowing what to expect. Through his child's eyes, the world was a cruel place in which he was always wrong.

In addition, John's parents would not let him make up his mind about even the smallest matters. They insisted that in every particular he ask them what he should do. Whenever he did anything on his own, he was usually punished for it, right or wrong, because he "should have asked first." Yet when he did ask his parents what he should do, their answers were inconsistent from one day to the next. And they never would give him reasons for their decisions: "Until you grow up, your parents are always right," they invariably said.

This sort of training follows the individual through life with unflagging tenacity. It makes it next to impossible for him to accomplish very much. As soon as one so trained is confronted with a situation which requires a decision, the old learned anxiety starts to churn and there is the automatic attempt to turn to someone else for the decision. But someone else is not always there.

Too many people in Madison reach out an arm in the morning, shut off the alarm clock, reach for a cigarette and light up. The cigarettes are there on the bedside table from the night before, when there was the need for a last cigarette before going to sleep.

Many people who smoke upon waking and before sleeping chain smoke during most of the day as well. They smoke when shaving, when working, and during meals. Suppose these people smoke two packs of king-sized cigarettes a day. This means that every day they smoke the equivalent of one long cigarette over ten feet in length: every year they smoke the equivalent of a cigarette well over two-thirds of a mile in length.

Young people usually begin to smoke because it is the thing to do. If a fellow does not, he is not really one of the gang.

At the beginning, he takes a cigarette to gain approval and to avoid disapproval. But when he puffs on a cigarette there is a momentary stimulation of the bodily processes—whether he inhales or not. Following that momentary stimulation the blood vessels become constricted. As a consequence the bodily processes slow down below normal. This slowing down reduces whatever tension there is in the body simply because the processes which cause the feeling of anxiety are slowed. Thus the reward of smoking is temporary reduction of anxiety. Smoking is a reward to the average person as well as to the extremely anxious one, for everyone has some need for reducing anxiety.

And what causes the anxiety? Mainly it is caused by the threat that our need to avoid disapproval will be frustrated. Will we get that raise so we can avoid the disapproval we feel is sure to come if we can't meet increased expenses and have to make do with a car that is not shiny enough and with a suit that is getting too shiny? Have another cigarette and reduce the anxiety while the question of the raise is in doubt.

What happens after one finishes a cigarette? The bodily processes speed up again. By contrast, they seem to be going faster than normal now. The processes churning up anxiety also seem to be moving faster than normal. There's one easy way to temporarily slow them down: reach for another cigarette.

Admittedly, smoking does temporarily alleviate anxious feelings due to threatening disapproval. But it is a poor way of avoiding these feelings because it harms the physical organism. Smoking makes the organism work harder to accomplish the same ends. This is why heavy smokers feel so tired out so much of the time. Also, it is likely that the tars in tobacco smoke act on the lung tissues and predispose them toward cancer.

Of course, the very anxiety which smoking reduces is also harmful to the organism. If that anxiety is not reduced it will disrupt the chemical balance of the body and make the body more susceptible to illness. So perhaps smoking is not quite the total evil it is sometimes made out to be.

The overeater is basically much like the chain smoker. He overeats to try to reduce anxiety. In the main the anxiety results from the threat of disapproval. The processes by which food is digested are such that the feeling of anxiety is temporarily alleviated.

But overeating is a poor way of trying to avoid the anxiety occasioned by the threat of disapproval because it leads to obesity, and obesity leads to further disapproval. As a result more anxiety develops. So the individual resorts to the habit of overeating to alleviate that added anxiety. The circle is most vicious.

It is extremely difficult for people to diet because the reward for doing so is so far in the future while the frustration is so much in the present. It's like giving up the better part of your weekly income now for a million dollars when you are eighty-four. It takes at least a few months for an obese person to lose an appreciable amount of weight. Meanwhile, he has to cope with hunger pangs and with the anxiety brought on by the real or imagined daily slings and arrows of disapproval. Usually, this is a little too much for him so he has a "small" snack.

A lawyer in Madison named Stephen Anderson is an example of another type who tries unsuccessfully to avoid disapproval. He is afflicted with one minor illness after another. These illnesses are real enough to him but they are brought on by tension. That is, they are psychosomatic illnesses. And the anxiety behind them is brought on by frustration of his need to avoid disapproval. Of course, Stephen Anderson is not aware of this. He just knows that he is constantly plagued with minor illnesses and he wishes he weren't.

Anderson is a big middle-aged man. He looks healthy enough. Unless you knew him very well, you'd never think he had been ill a day in his life. He is not a complainer, but he has terrible headaches a good deal of the time. His eyes tire quickly and they ache and sting a lot. There are periods when his stomach is severely upset. He has numerous lasting colds. Then there are the many ailments, each of which has occurred only once. One time Anderson had sharp pains in his right arm and shoulder which were so bad that he could not use his arm for a month. Another time he had a severe, highly irritating skin rash over most of his body for some weeks. Currently his heart is acting up on him; there are periods when it palpitates wildly.

Anderson has gone to doctors about several of these ailments. But they never seem to be able to put their finger on the cause of the trouble. Naturally, Anderson's capacity for work and recreation is reduced enormously.

He tries to take a philosophical view of his ailments. "There's always something wrong with me. I might as well accept it," he says, and then adds, "But I'll be damned if I can figure out why."

Are his ailments really related to a need to avoid disapproval? Isn't that a little farfetched? No, I don't think it is once you understand something of Stephen Anderson's total situation. The central reason why he is trying to avoid disapproval is that he feels himself to be pretty much of a failure. But how can that be when he's a lawyer with a respectable practice in Madison? It is because his goals were so much higher than those which he has achieved.

Anderson worked hard to put himself through a top law school. He wanted to be a big corporation lawyer. That was his ideal of success. Then he married a girl from Madison and, at her absolute insistence, settled down in Madison, so she could be near her family. He has become what people think of as a respected small-town lawyer. Madison's a big town now but that's how people think of him. And there is nothing wrong with that. People think well of him; they approve of him. But the important thing is not what people think of him, but what he *thinks* people think of him. If we are to understand an individual's behavior, we must see the situation from that individual's *subjective* point of view as well as from the objective viewpoint of an observer. Anderson assumes that people think he's a failure because he himself *feels* he is a failure, since he has not achieved his goal of a corporation lawyer. You must understand that this feeling of disapproval is real to him, as real as the scorn of a small community may be to, let us say, the newly-discovered adulteress.

The anxiety caused by the frustration of his need to avoid disapproval brings on Anderson's illnesses. On the one hand, it weakens his body so that he is more susceptible to illness. On the other hand, his particular illnesses are the ways his body "chooses" for trying to avoid the situation which causes the anxiety. They are, as it were, defenses which his body is trying to erect against his failure to reach his chosen goal of success. They are not defensive excuses which Stephen Anderson is consciously making for himself, but unconscious defenses which his organism is forced to throw up against the situation causing anxiety. In effect, his organism is trying to say: If I have terribly severe headaches, if my eyes are weak and ache, if my arm and shoulder pain me in the extreme, how can I be expected to accomplish more than I do?

Chapter 10

ODD AVOIDERS

PEOPLE develop innumerable unusual habits for trying to avoid disapproval. In Madison, for example, there is a housewife named Joan Travis who has a phobia of crowds of people and, in fact, of any public places where there are likely to be strangers. Recently Joan Travis walked down Highland Avenue, past the old gray mansions of an earlier day toward the center of Madison. It was a lovely morning. As she approached the intersection at the east end of Main Street, Joan Travis could feel the blood pumping inside her. She had to force herself to keep walking. The night before she had agreed with her husband that she should walk into Madison alone the next day. A package had to be mailed and she would take it to the post office.

"If you don't try, you'll never be able to manage in a crowd," her husband had said. "The more you avoid it, the worse it will get."

She had not been in a crowd without her husband for six months and had agreed that she should try it. Now, approaching Main Street, she thought what a fool she had been to think she was over it. She looked down Main Street. Three people were walking toward her along the right-hand sidewalk. No one was on the left-hand sidewalk except where the stores began several blocks further in toward the center of town. She crossed to the left side and started down Main Street.

It was hard to breathe. She expected herself to turn and run. But she kept on. This is silly, she thought, nothing can possibly happen to me. But it was still hard to breathe and the blood pounded steadily in her head and stomach.

She reached the point where the stores began. She walked steadily, not looking to either side. Two men came out of a store. She got past them; they went the other way. She kept her eyes focused on the post office, three blocks down. She kept repeating to herself, "Keep going." She knew that if she did not keep going she would turn and run wildly.

She kept on.

People came toward her, blurred, and passed by. The revolving doors of the post office were just ahead. The door was turning. She was in a segment of it and turned with the door.

She was inside. People were everywhere and she could not get out. She fainted.

Joan Travis' behavior seems rather extreme. You may wonder how she has managed to get along up to now. Generally, she has just avoided getting into crowd situations except when she has been with her husband. When she has been with him she has felt nervous but it has not been too bad.

But why did this phobia of Joan Travis' develop? And why is the anxiety decreased when she is with her husband? First of all, it is important to note that phobias are almost always learned in childhood. The child is badly frightened or made severely anxious in some way at one particular time or over a period of time. He develops a phobia of what frightened him, made him anxious or, in some cases, of something which was associated with what frightened him or made him anxious but which did not actually cause the fright or anxiety. (For example, he may develop a phobia of small rooms because he was severely frightened while in his small bedroom.) In either case the individual usually represses the remembrance of the original fright situation and all that remains is what appears to be an irrational fear of some object or situation.

Obviously not all phobias are motivated by the need to avoid disapproval. The need to avoid pain may be behind the phobia as is the case when a child is attacked by a dog and develops a phobia of animals. But Joan Travis' phobia of crowds is motivated by the learned need to avoid disapproval. Strangers in public places symbolize disapproval to her. Her early years were insecure ones. Her mother died when she was two. Her father's work required that he travel much of the time and so an elderly aunt brought her up. The aunt was a good woman but had outmoded ideas. She dressed Joan so that she looked more like a little old lady than a little girl. She seldom displayed any signs of outward affection for Joan although she did like the child. She was a stern woman and she disapproved of the slightest deviation from what she considered ladylike behavior. She never punished Joan physically but she would lock her in her room for long periods as punishment. Naturally Joan learned a strong need to avoid disapproval.

The aunt failed to teach Joan habits which she could use to avoid disapproval when she went to school. In fact, the things the aunt insisted she do were just the things which would lead to disapproval. For example, the aunt made her wear those old-fashioned clothes which the other children ridiculed. The aunt insisted that she take soup to school in a jar in her lunch box and the other children had great fun about the soup also.

When Joan was sixteen she went to her first dance, which was also her last until she met the man who is now her husband. Her aunt had been fiercely opposed to her going, but Joan had won the argument. The aunt made over an old but once stylish dress of her own for Joan. Well, the dress was a terrible affair. Joan had misgivings about wearing it but, you see, she had little to judge by except her aunt's standards. Oh, she realized it was different from the dresses the other girls wore, but her aunt said it was just the thing and Joan couldn't be sure it was not just the thing. Besides, it was a question of either wearing that dress or not going to the dance at all.

Joan went to the dance (it was a high-school dance) with a boy named Maurice Swan. When Maurice saw the dress, his Adam's apple bobbed rather rapidly but Joan's aunt told him his tie was crooked and then she shooed them off and into the town taxi which Maurice had waiting out front.

They got to the dance and after Joan had taken off her velvet wrap, it seemed to both her and Maurice that something was wrong. Everyone seemed to be so intent on watching them. Maurice kept looking around behind him as if he were afraid a huge tail had sprouted from the seat of his trousers. When they walked off the floor after the first dance, people stood in little groups watching them and making remarks to each other. By now it was clear to Joan that it was her dress which was attracting attention, and Maurice was no longer concerned about the possibility of a tail having sprouted from the seat of his pants.

Well, the dress was pretty bad. It looked like an old starched yellow kimono with pink spots on it. But it was tied in at the waist by a wide pink ribbon the ends of which hung down the back to ankle level.

Maurice Swan led Joan over near where some girls were standing together and he mumbled awkwardly about having to go somewhere and being back soon and then he disappeared. Joan did not see him again that evening because Maurice went out the back door of the high school and kept right on going.

Joan stood there and the other girls said nothing, feeling guilty for having laughed at her. The next dance began and the girls slid away. Joan stood alone; the faculty members watched her and did not know what to do. No one asked her to dance. She did not know many of the faculty well; she did not know many of the students well either; she felt as if she were trapped in a hostile camp of strangers and suddenly she bolted. She went out the door like a shot. When she got home she screamed and screamed. Her aunt was truly scared and telephoned the doctor who came and said it was a touch of nerves, that she must be upset about something, and gave her a sleeping pill.

That dance marked the beginning of the development of Joan's phobia of crowds of people. She started to high school the Monday following the dance, but when she reached the corner across the street from the school she could go no further. Some of her classmates were coming down the side street. She fled home.

Joan never returned to school. She felt that she simply could not face the students and teachers again, and her aunt did not insist that she continue in school. After several weeks at home Joan managed to find, through a friend of her aunt's, a job as a typist. But while at work she was always fearful that some of the students or teachers she knew would come into the office. This was highly unlikely but she was fearful nonetheless. Also, she was afraid she would meet them on the street going to and from work. The anxiety made it impossible for her to do her work. After less than a month she left the job.

Gradually Joan began to repress the memory of that school dance. It was never completely repressed, having occurred later in life than most situations which precipitate a phobia. But it was repressed to the extent that the thought of it never entered her consciousness except when someone mentioned it, which was seldom. At the same time, her anxiety about meeting the students and teachers who had been at the dance began to extend to going to public places and meeting people in general. She could no longer go downtown shopping. She could no longer go in public anywhere without experiencing an overwhelming fear, even though it was during school hours and impossible for the students or teachers to be there.

Having partially repressed the memory of the dance, Joan was no longer fully aware that her feelings were an extension of the anxiety caused by disapproval at the dance. She only knew that she felt terribly nervous and weak when she was out and that she had the uncontrollable urge to bolt for home. She and her aunt began to feel that her nervousness and weakness were due to some kind of vague ill health.

They both thought that it might be good for her to get out in the country for a while, so she went to visit an older cousin who lived in the upper part of the state. There were few people there and Joan felt much stronger and much more relaxed than she had in many months. She began to spend long visits at the home of her cousin.

For some years Joan seldom went out in public places and seldom saw anyone except a few close friends. Fortunately, when she was twenty, she met a boy who was quite the opposite of her and who fell in love with her. Joan was then visiting her cousin. There was a summer camp nearby. The boy was a counselor there and he just came up on her cousin's porch and started talking to her. He was sure of himself and very easy to talk to. Joan was quite nervous at first, but after five minutes he was talking to her like an old friend. A year later Joan and he were married.

Joan's nusband is so good at getting along with people that she has come to feel not too uncomfortable no matter where she goes as long as he is with her. She feels she can depend upon him; he is her social prop. She feels people will not disapprove of her when he is there. Also, she knows he loves her and approves of her. With this implicit support from her husband, she has reached the point where she can play a reasonably normal part in get-togethers with their friends. In fact, she is now only slightly anxious among these friends even when her husand is not there. But whenever she gets out among strangers without him the old overwhelming fear returns and she must escape. The threat of disapproval presses on her unbearably.

There is a good possibility that Joan could overcome her phobia. First, she would need at least limited psychiatric treatment which would bring to her consciousness the forces which led up to her phobia: her aunt's unintentional role in her development of a particularly strong need to avoid disapproval and in her lack of development of habits for avoiding that disapproval; and the precipitating dance situation, the memory of which she has partially repressed.

Having gotten these things out into the open, into her consciousness, Joan would then need to *gradually* enter crowd situations on her own. She and her husband should go in crowd situations together much more than they do. Then, for example, he should wait in the car while she goes into small stores by herself, then while she goes into larger stores and public places like the post office by herself. Gradually the fear of disapproval would be outweighed by the combined approval of her husband and herself. But this would be possible only if she first had a clear understanding of the forces which led up to, and resulted in, the phobia.

Emily Wilkes is another housewife in Madison who has unconsciously developed a peculiar habit for trying to avoid disapproval: she has a compulsion to achieve perfection in her housework. The Wilkeses live in Breezy Acres. Certainly Emily Wilkes is the neatest housewife in Breezy Acres and probably in all Madison.

The Wilkes' house is small, as are most of the houses

in Breezy Acres, and they have no children. But Emily Wilkes cleans from 8:00 A.M. to 10:00 P.M. six days a week with time out for shopping and dinner. Still, she feels she is always a little behind in trying to keep up with her cleaning.

In the morning after Emily Wilkes' husband leaves for work, she immediately washes the dishes and scours the cereal pan and the coffee pot very carefully. She rinses them three times. Then she leaves the kitchen and begins to clean the bathroom. (She cleans the kitchen thoroughly every evening after dinner.) She cleans the bathroom thoroughly every morning, scours the porcelain, and mops the tiled floor. This takes about an hour and a half.

Then Emily goes on to the two small bedrooms and the living room, cleaning each thoroughly. Many cleaning operations she performs three times. For example, she feels it necessary to vacuum clean all the rugs three times. She feels that this is the only way one can be sure of getting all the dirt out. The rugs get thin pretty quickly but that can't be helped.

Now you may think that all this is something of an exaggeration of what Emily Wilkes actually does every day. But it is not. She feels that she must do her cleaning in this way. If she did not do it in this way, she would feel terribly uncomfortable—as if her failure to do it in this way would lead to some nameless, dire consequence.

When she has finished cleaning the two bedrooms, she takes ten minutes out for a cup of soup and two crackers. When she finishes her soup, she washes the cup and spoon carefully, scours the pan she heated the soup in, rinses them all three times and is ready to tackle the living room. As she cleans the living room, she feels the pressure of time passing more quickly than she can work. There is still the shopping list to make, the shopping to do and dinner to prepare. She feels she can't possibly have dinner ready by six o'clock. But she will have it ready by six because if she doesn't, then she won't be able to start cleaning the kitchen at seven o'clock.

Emily finishes the living room and begins to take inventory of the food supplies. Every day she counts all the supplies, right down to the exact number of potatoes and onions on hand. Then she makes her detailed shopping list and goes to the corner grocery store. She shops carefully and then hurries home to prepare dinner.

After dinner, Emily does the dishes and cle— the kitchen from seven to ten while her husband reads in the living room. The kitchen is the biggest cleaning task in the house because there are so many appliances and utensils to be cleaned. She scours the stove and sink. She scours the utensils which she has used for dinner. She washes those which she hasn't used for dinner because she feels that things collect dirt from day to day even when they are not used. Lastly, she mops the kitchen floor.

About ten Emily joins her husband in the living room. Almost every evening just after ten she tells him that they really ought to have a smaller place, there is simply too much to do.

Yes, they should, he says, and always adds that they will as soon as they can find one. He knows they can't find a house much smaller and he realizes that his wife is a bit extreme about cleaning. But he feels that if she's happy cleaning like that, why then let her go ahead and do it.

Emily settles in her chair with her volume of condensed books from the book club and turns to where she stopped the night before. She goes right through the book from beginning to end reading every word, regardless of whether or not she is interested in any given condensation. She feels that that is the way to do it. She marks passages of particular interest with a red pencil. At ten-thirty she stops reading and with the red pencil notes the date alongside the last line she has read. It takes her a good six months to finish a volume. Presently she is three volumes behind.

Emily is tired. She pats her husband on the shoulder, he pats her hand, and she goes to prepare for bed—which takes exactly one hour.

People like Emily, who have compulsions to do certain things and are perfectionists, can't help themselves. If they do not do these things, they have a feeling of anxiety or dread that something will go wrong. They cannot explain these feelings but they feel that way and so they act as they do.

But why do habits such as Emily Wilkes' develop?

When Emily married her husband Ed ten years ago, she was in many ways sorry that she was doing so. Oh, he's all right, she thought, but she just did not want to settle down to a humdrum married life. On the one hand, she knew she could not do better. Ed was a good fellow and hard-working, and he would provide her with a good home. She realized she was not a particularly attractive girl and that she came from a poor family in Madison. If she didn't marry Ed, she might never have a chance again to do even nearly as well.

On the other hand, Emily had what are sometimes called dreams of glory. She wanted to lead a gay, wild life for a few years at least—like a movie star but on a smaller scale, Emily thought. Now this sounds pretty silly and a bit corny but, remember, these dreams of glory are sometimes very real and very serious to young people who have little. In one part of her mind, Emily knew she had no chance of leading a gay, wild life whether she married Ed or not. In another part of her mind, however, she could not give up the dreams and when there were no mirrors nearby she sometimes imagined herself as strikingly beautiful. But she married Ed, and they moved right into the little house in Breezy Acres which Ed had already bought.

Housework was about the last thing in the world Emily wanted to do. It symbolized everything which was in opposition to her dreams. But if she did not do it she and Ed would have no decent home. Their friends would disapprove of her thoroughly, and Ed might even throw her out. She felt she had no choice but to do the housework.

In the first few months of their marriage, these compulsive habits of Emily's began to develop. She did not develop them consciously. They came about as a defensive adjustment to a situation of conflict. She did not want to do housework but she was afraid of the disapproval she would encounter if she did not. So she overreacted, rigidly and extremely, as a means of trying to solve the conflict. The overreaction had to be rigid and extreme, compulsive and perfective, if it was to stand up under the pressure of her desires to lead a gay, wild life. In a sense, Emily's compulsive habits do work fairly well. They have lessened her conflict. She does not feel any great anxieties; she avoids disapproval, and she and Ed are certainly happier than if she did no housework.

Chapter 11
ESCAPISTS

OF THE MANY patterns of behavior which people develop under particular environmental conditions as ways of attempting to escape extreme anxiety caused by frustration, or fear of frustration, or the need to avoid disapproval, alcoholism and homosexuality are two of the most common.

Jim Morgan, a salesman in the sporting goods store in Madison, is one who has developed alcoholism as a way of trying to escape disapproval. Jim is in his late thirties. He is friendly but he does not like to talk about drinking. If you press the point, he will say that he drinks a lot, yes, but he can handle his liquor and, in fact, he is thinking of cutting down. He will tell you this in the evening. It is the mornings in Morgan's life which are particularly significant, however.

There is a clicking noise and Jim Morgan awakens immediately. The sunlight hits him in the face. He rolls to the wall. The wall shimmers out of place and he pulls the pillow over his eyes.

His wife drops the Venetian blind cord and comes toward him, looking very neat in a cotton print dress.

"You'd better get up, Jim," she says, just as he expected.

The pulsating in his stomach grows slowly and steadily faster.

"Jim—"

"Make some coffee, will you?" he says.

"I've made it."

He waits for her to leave.

She puts out her hand and then draws it back. "Jim—" She stops. Then she goes on, "Jim, you're going to kill yourself if you keep on like this."

He waits for her to leave. The throbbing in his stomach continues. His thoughts focus on his head and hands, and they immediately seem to grow enormous and spongy like the head and hands of monster balloons in a parade.

His wife goes quietly out of the room.

Dread of what he cannot remember rises in him.

"Oh, Jesus," Jim says and swings his feet to the floor. The sunlight hits him in the face sideways. He sits there.

Everything seems still.

Gradually, the feeling comes over him that he is losing control of himself. The pulsating in his stomach grows faster. He feels as if he is going to drop off the edge of the world. He starts to call his wife but then gets up unsteadily and goes to his dresser. He opens the drawer with his spongy hands and takes out a flat bottle, clumsily turns the top off, and drinks from it. Heat flows down his throat and spreads through his chest. The throbbing gradually subsides. Dread flaps out of range.

Jim steps into the bathroom, washes and dresses quickly. Then he looks around him, drinks quickly from the flat bottle again, and slips it into his back pocket.

In the kitchen his wife is looking out of the window. He sits down and pours the coffee with both hands.

His wife turns toward him.

He puts up his hand. "Don't start, please."

She sits down.

He drinks the coffee quickly. The aching throbbing in his stomach starts again. He goes back to the bathroom, drinks from the bottle, and puts it back in his back pocket.

He strides out and takes his hat from the hall closet. His wife says, "Jim—"

"I'm late already," he says and goes out to meet another day.

Jim Morgan, like all alcoholics, has learned to drink as a way of reducing the severe anxiety which he feels because of past frustration of a strong need to avoid disapproval. Alcohol temporarily loosens inhibitions and decreases tension in the body. But the aftereffects of alcohol, the hangover, cause an increase in anxiety. And usually the only available way to reduce the increased anxiety is by taking more alcohol. Thus a vicious circle is set up.

As is often the case with alcoholics, Jim Morgan's

parents were exceedingly strict. They disapproved of him much more than they approved of him and caused an extreme sensitivity to disapproval to develop in him. Jim's parents were good people and they loved their son but they showed little outward sign of affection. As a consequence, he was an insecure child.

As Jim grew up, his parents made quite a point of the evils of drink. They thought alcohol the sauce of the devil and drilled into their boy the folly of splitting a cup with the horned one. (Paradoxically, this strong emphasis on the evils of drink is often a part of the alcoholic's early environment.)

Jim did not have a drink until he was twenty-two, at which time he had not only one but one too many as well. He was a member of a semiprofessional baseball club and a few of the boys liked to have a little party now and then; it was the thing to do. Jim, being particularly sensitive to disapproval, wanted to do the accepted thing.

He joined in and felt guilty about doing so because of his parents' lecturing about the evils of drink. He unwittingly had a few more drinks to assuage his guilt. They carried him home, and the next morning he felt worse than he ever had in his life. Not only did his head ache horribly and his stomach seem adrift of its moorings; all day he could not shake off the feeling that he had done something terribly wrong—something much more wrong than just having had too much to drink. He had not done anything wrong but he felt he had. It was his parents' disapproving voice multiplied ten times by the nerve-grating effects of the hangover.

Jim vowed never to have too much to drink again, if any at all. And during the next year, he took a drink occasionally but only so the boys would not think him other than a regular fellow.

Jim had wanted to be a ball player since his grammar school days. In high school, he had been the best player the school had ever had and he had achieved some fame in the area. Now, at twenty-three, he had a promising baseball career ahead of him. He was an outfielder for a popular semiprofessional team. He was good and he was improving fast. The next year he joined a minor league club and he looked like major league material. He married a girl from Madison, his home town; the future looked wonderful. He was on the road to approval and he was happy.

Then, two months after Jim joined the minor league club, he and his wife were driving home in their new car. Something off to the side of the road attracted his attention, he veered to the left, and collided with an oncoming car. Jim was the only one badly hurt—his shoulder was smashed. That was the end of his baseball career.

Jim and his wife went home to Madison and he got a job with the sporting goods store. That was almost fifteen years ago. The drop from a rising ballplayer to a salesman's job was a terrible blow to him. He had had almost unlimited approval in his grasp, and now disapproval stared him in the face. To Jim, with his strong sensitivity to disapproval, selling in a store with little future ahead of him was, relatively speaking, a position that could only put him in a disapproving light in the eyes of the world. But it was the only job he could get.

He did not start drinking heavily right after the accident. He tried to make the best of things. He had a drink now and then. Sometimes he had one too many, but that did not happen often at first. He did notice, however, that he always felt a great deal better when he had a drink or two. As a rule he felt rather depressed but a drink or two made everything look much brighter. He got terrible hangovers if he drank too much but there was no need to drink too much, he thought.

As the years went on, Jim felt he was getting nowhere. No one actually disapproved of him; but he felt that the world in general did and he disapproved of himself. His anxiety increased.

Gradually he took to having a few cocktails before dinner and a few drinks after dinner every day because they made him feel so much better. What they did was to decrease his anxiety and to lower, temporarily, his standards of what constituted disapproval; thus, they alleviated his feelings of disapproval.

Jim's wife thought this increased drinking a very bad habit and repeatedly told him so. He began to go out in the evenings and drink at bars. Then, a few years ago, he started drinking in the morning. He would wake up feeling so bad he couldn't make it to the store. He had a drink and it did wonders for him temporarily.

But it soon wore off and he needed another to keep going.

Now, he needs a drink constantly to keep going. He can't break the circle because there is nowhere to begin. It has come to the point where Jim always gets to the store late. Sometimes in the afternoons the customers have a feeling there is something wrong with him. The owner of the store knows Jim drinks on the job and has spoken to him about it but to no avail. Much as he likes Jim, he is about to let him go.

The pattern of development of most alcoholics is much like Jim's. There is no concrete evidence that there is any inherited predisposition in the physical make-up toward alcoholism. The causes seem to be greatly environmental. And the early environment is of great importance in setting the stage. As in Jim's case, the pattern is usually that of a strict childhood with the parents outwardly expressing little love, disapproving of the child more than approving of him and making an issue of the evils of drink. In cases where one parent of the alcoholic has been a heavy drinker, the other parent has usually made an issue of the evils of drink. Alcoholism seldom afflicts individuals from homes where mild drinking was accepted as a normal part of life.

In any case, the potential alcoholic feels vaguely unloved and insecure as a child and has a strong need to avoid disapproval. The emphasis on the evils of drinking makes him feel guilty later if and when he does take a drink to avoid the disapproval of his friends. So he drinks more to assuage the guilt. Because of the guilt his hangover symptoms are accentuated. Eventually these severe hangovers play a part in the development of morning drinking—the hallmark of approaching alcoholism.

The alcoholic is always one who drank moderately for a period, usually during his twenties. Then if he is faced with continual minor frustrations of his need to avoid disapproval, or with one or more major frustrations, he turns to increased drinking as a way of reducing the consequent anxiety. Morning hangovers, laden with pain, guilt and increased anxiety, lead him to round-the-clock drinking and he passes into the stage of chronic alcoholism, usually in his late thirties or early forties.

Of course, some people become alcoholics even though

they are not faced with any apparent frustrations of their need to avoid disapproval. They become successful in their work, may even achieve a measure of fame, and yet they become alcoholics. In these cases, the individuals *feel* the disapproval of others upon them nonetheless. They take what success they achieve for granted and they assume, more or less unconsciously, that people disapprove of them in everyday relationships. They feel inadequate in their social relationships in spite of their occupational success. This feeling results in frustration of their need to avoid disapproval. Then if they have had the early environmental background mentioned above, they turn to alcohol as a means of relieving the anxiety caused by the frustration.

Since the alcoholic's need to avoid disapproval has invariably been frustrated, he also has a need to aggress. (As will be discussed in the next chapter, frustration always leads to a need to aggress.) Sometimes excessive drinking is directed toward satisfying the need to aggress as well as toward trying to escape the anxiety of disapproval. Thus some who drink lose their inhibitions about aggressive behavior and become verbally or physically offensive. On the other hand, many who drink excessively do not become aggressive. Jim Morgan is one who does not. A case can be made for the point that he and all alcoholics are always aggressing against themselves by their drinking—unconsciously tearing down their systems, slowly killing themselves. But in the main, and certainly in Jim Morgan's case, it is the need to escape the anxiety of disapproval which motivates excessive drinking rather than the need to aggress.

There are two types of cures for alcoholism. The first is by the aid of Alcoholics Anonymous, whose members and social programs help by moral support and kindness to reduce the individual's anxiety and feelings of disapproval. The second cure is by lengthy psychiatric treatment. This is the only complete cure because it can get at the root of the trouble and reduce the learned need to avoid disapproval. But such treatment is costly. Also the alcoholic will seldom admit that he needs psychiatric help. He unconsciously tries to avoid getting into such a situation because he will be required to give up the one defense which he has against the pain of anxiety. He feels he has no real assurance that psychiatric treatment will actually reduce the anxiety.

Above all, the alcoholic should be treated with kindness; he needs affection. Strange as it may seem, he usually cannot by himself break the vicious circle and stop drinking.

The homosexual is a second type whose behavior is directed toward escaping the anxiety which disapproval brings. The behavior of the homosexual is severely disapproved by most of society, it is true. But that disapproval causes less anxiety for the homosexual than does the fear of disapproval which he or she experiences when in contact with sexually capable members of the opposite sex. This fact is evident in the case of James Finch, a young man who has been a practicing homosexual for some years.

James Finch is blond and good-looking in a fragile way; he is always very carefully dressed. One evening recently he sat at the bar in the end of the cocktail lounge of the Madison Pickwick Arms Hotel sipping his drink.

A woman came up to the bar and carefully settled on the stool beside him. He did not know her, and he did not want to know her so he looked the other way.

"Have a drink on me," the woman said.

James Finch looked at her. Her glass tipped in her hand. She drank and a trickle ran down her chin from the left corner of her mouth.

James Finch looked away. He inhaled slowly on his cigarette, his head averted.

"I said have a drink on me," the woman said.

"Please go away immediately," James said.

The woman stared at him. The glass tipped in her hand and then she said, "Oh, one of that kind."

He picked up his change, slid off the stool and went out the door fast.

The woman nodded to the bartender and said, "He's one."

Outside, James Finch stepped into the only taxi in front of the Madison Pickwick Arms and gave an address. He felt as if he had just escaped from an airless room. He tried to get his breath.

Soon the taxi stopped at the address Finch had given, a small apartment house on the edge of Madison. He paid the driver, went into the building quickly, up to the second floor, rang a bell by one of the doors, and waited.

A big man opened the door. "Why, James, it is so nice to see you," he said.

"George, I've just had the most frightful experience," James said.

"Come in, dear boy, and tell Georgie all about it," George said to him, smiling.

He went in and George closed and locked the door behind him.

Before considering why James Finch has developed as he has, several points should be made clear. First, the homosexual is one who has repeated, exclusive sexual relationships with members of his own sex. Effeminate habits in men and masculine habits in women do not necessarily indicate homosexuality. Some individuals have the mannerisms of those of the opposite sex but do not have sexual relationships with those of their own sex.

As seems to be true of alcoholism, homosexuality is not inborn—it is learned. The homosexual's extreme anxiety about members of the opposite sex is due to severe disapproval by members of that sex in early life. Because of this extreme anxiety, the individual cannot have sexual relationships with them, but he still has a need for sexual outlet. So he turns to members of his own sex, with whom he does not experience anxiety.

James Finch's history runs briefly along the following line. His mother was a disapproving, domineering woman who dominated his father right out of the home. The father left when James was four and has not been heard from since by either James or his mother. Following that, she dominated her son completely. He was truly afraid of her. This laid the groundwork for his later anxiety in the presence of women. As an adolescent in high school he was exceedingly timid and the girls ridiculed him. So did the boys, for that matter.

In his late teens and early twenties James had a strong need for sexual outlet as do most males of that age. But he felt exceedingly nervous with girls because, partly unconsciously and partly consciously, he feared their disapproval. He associated all females with his mother, and he wanted to avoid repetition of the humiliating experiences in high school. As a result, he simply could not bring himself to go out with girls. The threat of their disapproval was too strong.

Then James met George, the man to whose apartment he went from the Madison Pickwick Arms. George was an older man and a practicing homosexual. He was kind to James and James found a way of satisfying his own need for sexual outlet.

By having sexual relationships with members of the same sex, the homosexual gets a triple reward. He satisfies his need for sexual outlet, he escapes the threat or fact of face-to-face disapproval by those of the opposite sex, and he often gains considerable approval from his homosexual partner.

On the other side of the ledger is the fact that the homosexual is highly disapproved of by society in general. But the rewards he gets for his homosexual behavior tend to outweigh the frustration caused by this disapproval by society, and so his homosexual behavior continues. However, he is almost always in a state of conflict: the demands of society weigh upon him heavily. Because of this perpetual state of conflict many homosexuals become neurotic.

The homosexual's learned anxiety in the face of members of the opposite sex is so strong that it is highly unlikely that he can develop normal sexual habits, even with psychiatric help. Each time he tries to associate with members of the opposite sex his anxiety will in all probability lead them to hold him in low regard. The situation will seem as hopeless as ever to him.

PART IV

AGGRESSION APPROVAL AND DISAPPROVAL

Juvenile Delinquent: Society is purposely against him ...

WHEN ANY NEED of the physical organism is frustrated, another need invariably arises—the need to aggress—according to an idea developed by John Dollard and his associates in *Frustration and Aggression* (Yale University Press, 1939). Thus when the individual's need for approval or for avoiding disapproval is frustrated, he feels the need to aggress. Basically, the need to aggress is not learned; it is instinctive. It is analogous to the aggression aspect of the Freudian id. But the particular nature of the behavior the individual employs to try to satisfy this need will depend on his learning in his earlier environment. Broadly speaking, the nature of his behavior will depend on the degree to which the individual was socialized as a child—the degree to which he was taught and learned the ways of acting which are acceptable to society, the degree to which he learned the conscience aspect of the Freudian superego. If he was socialized well but not overly so, he will tend to aggress in ways which are fairly acceptable to society and not harmful to himself. For example, he may argue a lot, a verbal form of aggression which, if kept within bounds, is reasonably acceptable or at least not particularly unacceptable.

If the individual has been oversocialized, he will tend to be afraid of acting in any outwardly aggressive way; it might not be fully acceptable. Instead, he will aggress against himself. The most extreme example here would be suicide.

If however, the individual has been undersocialized as a child—has not been taught and learned to do things in a reasonably acceptable way—then he will, if frustrated, tend to aggress against other people in ways which are altogether unacceptable. He may pop someone in the nose, or, to take the most extreme example, he may commit murder.

As we shall see, individuals sometimes act in ways which are attempts to satisfy, at the same time, the need to aggress and either the need to gain approval or the need to avoid disapproval. At other times they may act in ways which are attempts to satisfy at the same time all three needs. Finally, they may act in ways which are directed solely toward trying to satisfy the need to aggress. In the following chapters, we will consider, in turn, each of these three possibilities.

Chapter 12

VERBALIZERS

PEOPLE frequently develop verbal habits which allow them to vent their aggression in reasonably acceptable ways and to gain approval or avoid disapproval at the same time.

For example, arguing is a verbal habit which often yields some satisfaction of both the needs to aggress and to gain approval. One of the most accomplished arguers in Madison is John Groats, a youngish junior executive. Most people agree that he will argue about practically anything. Here is a fairly typical instance of Groats in action.

The conversation is flowing smoothly in one of the ranch houses in the Glenhaven section of Madison when John Groats enters with his quiet wife. John sits down in the nearest chair and listens, puffing at his pipe. He always starts out that way.

Harry Walker has just returned from a trip to West Germany and has been talking about the German economy. "Well, as I was saying," Walker goes on, "the Germans have really gotten on their feet. What they've accomplished in the past ten years is simply unbelievable. And, say what you will, like them or not, it's all due to the innate German capacity and desire for hard, efficient work."

"Oh, I wouldn't say that." It is John Groats making his conversational gambit.

"Beg your pardon?" says Harry Walker. He does not know John Groats very well.

"I wouldn't say that at all," repeats John Groats. He knocks the ashes from his pipe.

"You didn't find Germany that way?" Harry Walker asks him.

"I never visit countries I'm interested in," says John Groats, shaking his head. "Destroys your perspective. But to get back to your statement. You miss the point entirely. You see—"

"John, please," says John Groat's wife. She knows Harry Walker considers himself, and some others consider him, a sort of minor expert on Germany.

"You miss the point completely there, fellow," John Groats goes on. "You see, it has nothing to do with innate capacity. Do you really believe that the capacity to work efficiently or otherwise is ever inborn?"

"Well, I won't quibble over whether it's inborn or not," Harry Walker says, "I'm simply saying that every German *has* this capacity for efficient work and—"

"*Every* German?" says John Groats.

"Yes, practically every German has—"

"Now, look, fellow. There's a whale of a difference between every German and practically every German. I'm not trying to argue the point with you, I'm simply explaining to you—"

"Now, boys, let's keep it light," someone says.

"It's not important anyway," Harry Walker says.

"You're wrong there." John Groats is just warming up. "You see, this matter of the German character is actually one of the most important problems with which we are confronted today. Centrally, it's a question of—"

"Pardon me. I have to get a refill," Harry Walker says and gets up quickly.

Someone else in the group says, "I was down looking at Bill Johnson's house yesterday. Never cared much for these modern houses, but this place of his really makes sense."

"I wouldn't say that," says John Groats. "To begin with it is not actually modern. You see—" He puffs twice, quickly, on his pipe and then really warms up to the task at hand.

One time you'll find John Groats arguing one side of a question and another time you'll find him arguing the opposite side. He doesn't care which side he takes as long as it's the other one.

John's arguing is directed toward trying to simultaneously satisfy his needs to aggress and to gain approval. His need for approval is frustrated, not severely, but enough to cause in him a moderately strong need to aggress. His arguing is definitely a verbal form of aggression. He is always trying to put the other fellow in the wrong, make him seem somewhat stupid. At the same time, arguing is a fairly acceptable method of aggressing if not carried too far. It is not viewed with severe disapproval as is physical aggression. People get tired of it, yes, but they seldom strongly disapprove of it. Furthermore, some people approve of it as a means of intellectual stimulation, which it sometimes is. Consequently, John Groats now and then gains some approval from his arguing. True, he overestimates and thinks he gains more approval than he actually does. But what he thinks is what counts to him.

John began to develop the arguing habit when he was an adolescent as a way of trying to cope with what was for him a frustrating situation. John had an older brother whom his parents considered to be a paragon. The brother was in fact quite an adolescent success in certain ways. He was president of the junior class in high school, he was a straight "A" student, and he was a star on the football team. He thought he could do no wrong and his parents agreed with him. One could hardly blame John for disagreeing—which he did.

John was an average enough boy. He did fairly well in school, but people always seemed to be comparing him to the older brother. By comparison, John looked pretty hopeless. The brother got the lion's share of approval. John's need for a spot of the limelight was frustrated and he began to feel a need to aggress.

The older brother was always making self-assured statements around the house which John's parents took as gospel. He did the same outside the home. A lot of the things the brother said would not particularly hold water but he said them with such assurance that people accepted them without examining them closely. John, however, examined them closely and he took to pointing out their weaknesses to the older brother and to anyone else who was on hand. His parents and the older brother deplored this. But as a matter of fact, John was often right. He often succeeded in making the older brother look a bit foolish. That was all John needed. He took to disagreeing with everything the brother said. John worked off some aggression and he got some approval from people outside the family who were beginning to think the older brother was just a little too big for his breeches. The foundation of John's arguing habit was thus firmly laid.

Since those early adolescent days when his brother

got most of the approval, John has always been somewhat on the defensive. He still feels, as it were, that he is not gaining his share of approval. Whenever he sees someone seemingly gaining approval for speaking at all authoritatively on any given subject, the old aggressive feelings come over him and he resorts, for better or for worse, to the technique which worked against his brother.

A house on Chestnut Street shelters a lady, Mrs. Samuel Grull by name, who has another habit directed toward venting a little aggression and gaining a little approval: the habit of complaining. Chestnut Street, right in the city of Madison, is one of those streets where slightly rundown two-family houses predominate. The house on the corners stands out from the others, however. It has been newly painted a mustard yellow and it is a one-family house. The big screened porch extends almost to the sidewalk. The house is ugly but neat.

Mr. and Mrs. Grull have lived in this house for twenty years. There is Mrs. Grull, a round woman, and Mr. Grull, a man of few words. With them live their daughter Edna and her new husband, Sydney Powell. The young folks have a newly decorated apartment upstairs just until they can find exactly what they want.

It is after dinner. The two Grulls and the two Powells sit on the front porch.

"It's terrible hot," says Mrs. Grull fanning herself with the society page of *The Madison Times-Herald*.

"Yes, it is, Mother," says Edna. "Isn't it, Sydney?"

"Yes, it certainly is," Sydney says.

"Just right," Mr. Grull says from behind the sports page. Smoke curls slowly up from his pipe.

"You don't have to make dinner," says Mrs. Grull.

Mr. Grull does not answer.

"I could melt away in that kitchen and no one would care."

"Mother, of course we care," says Edna. "I'd help you, but we agreed I'd do the cleaning and you'd—"

"It doesn't matter. It doesn't matter. I'm just the hired woman around here."

"Mother!"

"I never thought the day would come when—"

"Oh, for Christ sakes, shut up!" says Mr. Grull from behind the sports page of *The Madison Times-Herald*.

Mrs. Grull takes a sharp breath, sniffles, gets up and goes into the house. "I never thought the day would come—"

Edna follows her.

Mrs. Grull seeks sanctuary in the dimness of the parlor. Edna sits down beside her.

Suddenly Mrs. Grull looks up and, peering at Edna, says, "Why does he hate me?"

"Who? Why does who hate you, Mother?"

"You know who. Sydney. Why does he hate me so?"

"Why, Sydney doesn't hate you, Mother. He loves you."

"He hates me. He hardly ever says a word to me."

"He's just quiet, Mother."

"Why doesn't he speak to me? Why does he hate me so?"

"But, Mother, Sydney doesn't hate you. You're just upset about dinner. From now on I'll help you and—"

"No. You'll be leaving me. I know. You and him looked at a house yesterday, didn't you?"

"Why yes, we did, Mother. But you know we planned to buy as soon as we could find a nice little house."

"After all I've done for you. I just don't understand it. I just don't understand it at all."

"Sadie!" It is Mr. Grull calling his wife. "Sadie. Where the hell's the rest of the paper?" Mr. Grull wants the funnies on the back of the women's page of *The Madison Times-Herald*.

Mrs. Grull gets up and goes out to the porch. "I don't even have time to look at the paper."

She gives Mr. Grull the part of the paper with which she has been fanning herself and he takes it wordlessly.

"Oh, it's so hot," says Mrs. Grull, sitting in her rocker once again. "I'll never live the summer out."

"It is awfully hot, Mother," says Edna.

"If we had a house outside of town, it wouldn't be so hot," says Mrs. Grull, slowly fanning her face with her hand. "Samuel, why don't we buy out in Breezy Acres? Or maybe even Beauty Hills?"

Her husband does not seem to hear.

"Why don't we, Samuel? Don't you care about me at all?"

"You'd find something wrong out there, too," says Mr. Grull from behind the newspaper.

"I certainly would not. We'd have neighbors that amounted to something out there. Not like the riffraff here."

"It's just as hot there as here," Mr. Grull says.

"You're at work all day. In a nice cool plant," says Mrs. Grull. "You don't have to broil in this hot box all day."

Mr. Grull, with considerable puffing, gets up, pads into the house, goes to the refrigerator for a can of beer, opens it, and pads upstairs to bed.

"Time for bed, Edna," says Sydney Powell and he, Edna and Mrs. Grull get up and go inside.

"I'll bring your lemonade up, children," says Mrs. Grull.

"Thank you, Mother. That would be nice," says Edna, and she and Sydney go up to their apartment.

Soon Mrs. Grull knocks on their door. Edna says, "Come in, Mother."

Mrs. Grull enters carrying a tray with two glasses of lemonade and four cookies on it. She looks very sad. She puts the tray on the bedside table, says "Good night, children," and then turns toward the door.

"What's the matter, Mother?" Edna says.

"Oh, it's nothing," answers Mrs. Grull. She continues slowly toward the door.

"What is it, Mother?"

"Oh, nothing. Nothing. I wish someone would bring me some lemonade, just once," says Mrs. Grull.

"But, Mother—"

"Good night, children," says Mrs. Grull and closes the door behind her.

"Poor Mother," says Edna. "She's so sensitive. What can be wrong with her?"

"Too much lemonade," says Sydney who, as a married man of twenty-two, prefers a glass of beer.

Well, Mrs. Grull's complaining is an unconscious habit she has developed as an attempt to satisfy her need for approval and her need to aggress, the latter having arisen as a result of frustration of the former.

The frustration of Mrs. Grull's need for approval is due to her relatively low position in the community and to her lack of material belongings, the possession of which stands for approval to her. Mrs. Grull's husband is a day laborer, they live in one of the less desirable sections of Madison, and they have a fifteen-year-old car and worn furniture. She feels that because of these facts she is denied the approval she deserves. She has always dreamed of serving tea in grand style in a rose garden and here she is living right in town in an old and ugly house and her husband on the front porch in his undershirt with a can of beer.

Mrs. Grull feels the need "to cut a fancy figure" in Madison. Since she does not do so, she feels she is not getting the approval of others. And she is somewhat right. The Grulls are not looked upon with much approval by the other people of Madison. Like many people in their walk of life they are neither approved of nor disapproved of.

Mrs. Grull's need for approval is obviously not satisfied in any degree by her husband, either. He used to give her a measure of approval but he has long since given that up. In the early days of their marriage he used to boast, to Mrs. Grull's delight, that "Sadie is full of beans and a yard wide." But Mr. Grull soon concluded that any such scraps of approval which he tossed out only created in Mrs. Grull an insatiable appetite for more of the same. So now he confines his comments to the fact that "she's gettin' wider all the time."

Because of the frustration of her need for approval Mrs. Grull feels vaguely aggressive toward her family and the world in general. Over the years she unconsciously nurtured the habit of complaining to her family and to others as a way of more or less acceptably venting her aggression and of gaining approval as well. The habit is acceptable in the sense that there is usually some semblance of truth in the things she complains about.

Mrs. Grull's complaining satisfies her need to aggress because it does hurt the members of her family, annoy them, and make them uncomfortable. She annoys Mr. Grull. And she definitely hurts her daughter, Edna, who is made to feel guilty for not being better to her mother although objectively the girl is all that a daughter should be. Mrs. Grull's complaining causes trouble between Edna and Sydney. Edna feels that they should do what her mother complains they don't do, and Sydney feels they should do what he wants to do.

Mrs. Grull unconsciously "realizes" this. She would not consciously hurt her family, but this is the kind of thing with which she can get away without worrying her conscience. She feels fine after a good session of complaining because she has vented her aggression.

The habit leads to some approval as well. Not from Mr. Grull it is true and not from Sydney either. But from Edna she gains quite a measure of a sympathetic sort of approval. Edna feels she has to agree with her mother when the latter specifies the nature of the burdens she bears. Edna feels compelled to tell her mother that yes, she does work too hard, that she must not work so hard, that she is the best mother in the world and so on.

It is often said that complainers like Mrs. Grull are only happy when they are complaining. There is a good deal of truth in this. They are satisfying their needs and so they are happy. If the habit were not rewarding, it would not thrive so heartily.

A third type of behavior which is directed toward both aggressing and attempting to gain approval is gossiping. Sometimes you can discover just a few faint traces of gossip riding the waves of conversation when three or four of the ladies of Madison get together for a few hours relaxation at the card table.

Last Friday, Leda Cole and Catherine Smith were at Helen Sheppard's in Glenhaven and Helen said, "I'm afraid we'll have to play canasta, girls. Sally called up a little while ago and said she couldn't come."

"Did she say why she couldn't come?" Leda asked.

"Said she didn't feel well."

"Oh. That's too bad," Catherine said. "I wonder if there's anything we can do for her." Catherine is twenty-two and the newest member of the Glenhaven set.

"Well, under the circumstances it's best not to ask. Might embarrass her," Leda said. "Of course you've heard—" She stopped and waited to be sure the others had not heard. Leda was one of the charter members of the Glenhaven set.

"Heard what, Leda?" Helen said.

"Oh, I thought you knew. I never would have mentioned it but I thought you knew by now." Leda glanced quickly to one side and then leaned over the table. "Well, don't repeat this and don't tell a soul I told you. Sally is pregnant."

"Oh, how nice," Catherine said.

"Oh, no, my dear. Not nice. Not nice at all. You've missed the point entirely, I'm afraid. Didn't you know her husband has only been back from that engineering job for two weeks?"

"Oh, I see. Well, maybe—"

"Leda, are you sure?" Helen said. "I simply don't believe that she—"

"Well, naturally, she didn't come right out and tell me if that's what you mean, dear," Leda said. "But I noticed last week that she wasn't looking well. And then the next day she hung out the wash much later than usual. So I decided I'd drop over for some coffee and see if she was all right. And do you know, she was just sitting there in a chair, the breakfast dishes weren't even washed, and she looked positively green. There's no doubt about it—she's pregnant."

"But, Leda, I don't see that that necessarily means she's pregnant," Helen said. "She might just—"

"Have I ever been wrong about something like this? Besides, I happened to drop over to Connie Bates' right afterward and Connie said she's noticed queer things about Sally lately too and that she'd been thinking the same thing I had. We both couldn't be wrong. Of course, Connie is an awful gossip, we all know that, but she doesn't miss a thing and you can hardly blame her for being a gossip with all the trouble she's had."

"Shall we draw for the deal?" Helen said. She spread the cards out on the table. They each took a card.

"Your deal, Leda," Helen said.

Leda began to shuffle the cards, slowly. "Poor Connie," she said. "It must be awful. That husband of hers—you know how I hate gossip and I wouldn't breathe a word of this to anyone but you and Catherine—but that husband of hers— Well, one night last week Caroline Johnson's sister was in a little bar in the city and she's sure she saw Jim Bates there at a corner table with the most awful looking peroxided blonde. And all this time poor Connie thinks Jim is going to night school. Of course she doesn't do a thing to fix herself up, you can hardly blame him I suppose, but still, after all—" Leda put down the cards and patted her new hairdo. "But on the other hand, Connie has other things to worry about, I suppose. Caroline Johnson says that little boy of Connie's is a half-wit at best."

"What a shame," Catherine said.

"I wondered about it myself," Leda said, "when I never saw him out playing with the other children and he's always so quiet when you go over there." She took out a cigarette and started looking in her handbag for a match.

"I'll get some matches and ashtrays," Helen said. "Go ahead and deal. I'll be right back." She went into the kitchen.

"Heavens, I never should have mentioned half-wits in front of Helen," Leda said to Catherine. "You know they say that Helen's brother—he's never been quite right, you know. Of course, Helen never talks about it but things like that do get around. Mary Danforth says he—I wouldn't dream of talking behind Helen's back, she's my dearest friend, but there are some things you simply can't say to a person's face—Mary Danforth says—"

"Well, I guess we're all set now," Helen said, coming from the kitchen with the ashtrays.

"Tell you later," Leda said to Catherine. "Why, Helen, what lovely little ashtrays. I never saw these before." Then she picked up the cards again and began to deal.

Leda goes on like this, gossiping about one person after another, because by downing others she works off a little aggression and has a feeling, at least, of gaining a little approval. Gossiping is a mild, acceptable form of aggression whereby she hurts others' reputations. And, by making others seem worse, she makes herself seem better in her own eyes. Also she gets what seems to her to be some approval from those to whom she gossips because they are interested in what she has to say. After all, who can turn his back on a nice piece of gossip? People listen to Leda, more or less admit she is on the inside track; and it makes her feel important.

As is the case with many extreme gossips, Leda leads a rather empty life. She has material security, but she has no children and her husband is away on business a lot of the time. She has no particular abilities which might win her approval. She is not particularly good-looking. She has nothing which makes it possible for her to enjoy, at least now and then, "a place in the sun." In order to work off a little of the consequent aggression and to gain what approval she can, she has developed the habit of gossiping to the point where it is fully automatic.

A fourth verbal type whose behavior is directed toward venting aggression is the disquieting fellow who has a knack for making you feel uncomfortable, for making you feel you've hurt his feelings when you really haven't done anything at all. But unlike the arguer, the complainer, and the gossip, he is not trying to gain your approval at the same time that he works off a little aggression. He is trying, rather, to avoid your disapproval.

One of those fellows with a knack for making you uncomfortable lives just down the street from us. We haven't been able to get to know him very well. Of course, we haven't tried very hard, but I don't suppose we would have gotten to know him very well even if we had tried. Take the other evening, for example, I turned from closing the garage door and he was standing there.

"Hello, Stanley," I said.

He stood his ground and coughed. "I don't suppose you'd want to give me a lift into town in the morning," he said solemnly.

"Why sure, Stanley, I'd be glad to."

"You don't have to," he said.

"What?" I asked him. I wasn't sure I understood.

"My car broke down but—you don't have to if it's too much trouble."

"It's no trouble, Stanley. The only thing is I have to be in town at eight-thirty tomorrow, so if you can be ready by—"

"Never mind, I'm sorry I asked."

"No, no. I'll be glad to give you a lift. It's just that I have to be in town at eight-thirty. What time do you usually leave in the morning?"

He was pointed toward his house. "About eight," he said.

"Well, that's when I'll be leaving anyway," I said. "No trouble at all."

"I can take the bus."

"No, Stanley, really, it's no trouble."

"It doesn't matter. Just forget about it."

"But I'll be glad to pick you up at eight."

He was still pointed toward his house but he nodded toward my garage. "How's the new car?"

"Oh, fine. Fine."

He nodded to himself and said, "Hmm." Somehow or other he succeeded in making me feel that there was something sinful about my having bought a new car.

Then he started off toward home.

"See you in the morning, Stanley," I said.

"Well, if it's any trouble, just forget about it. It really doesn't matter," he said as he started doggedly toward home. Then he added, over his shoulder, "I can always take the bus."

Now, this fellow Stanley is fairly well educated and has a good job. There is nothing in his immediate situation for him to be defensive about. But every time I run into him he displays this knack for making me feel vaguely like a heel for no apparent reason at all. He does this regardless of whether he is asking a favor. The other neighbors tell me he acts the same way with them, which always makes me feel a little better.

The truth of the matter is, Stanley is pretty aggressive underneath that stolid exterior of his. He is also quite concerned about avoiding any possibility of face-to-face disapproval. By making other people vaguely uncomfortable, by making other people feel that they have somehow or other slighted him, Stanley works off a little aggression. At the same time, he avoids the possibility of disapproval because they are kept busy trying to figure out why he seems to be disapproving of them.

After Stanley graduated from high school he had no money for college, so he took a clerking job and worked for eight years at a low salary. He went to night school and eventually earned a college degree. During those eight years he lived alone, worked very hard, and had little time for relaxation. He was not getting approval from anyone; his approval lay in the future. He felt frustrated and envious of those who led a happier life. He developed feelings of aggression toward other people in general and he still has those feelings. It is true that he is no longer frustrated in his need for approval. He has a good job now, is married, and has a nice home. But the old feeling hangs on.

Stanley's disquieting ways are directed toward getting rid of some of that aggression in an acceptable manner. They are not directed toward gaining approval; he has that now. But he is trying to avoid disapproval as well as to release his aggression. This need to avoid disapproval concerns another aspect of Stanley's personality which we have not touched upon. He has always been a person who was awkward and stiff in social situations because he feared disapproval. This very awkwardness and stiffness brought him some mild disapproval in earlier years. He unconsciously developed his disquieting habits as ways of diverting attention from his awkwardness and uncertainty. His habits force other people to direct their attention toward whatever they may have said or done which seems to have slighted him rather than toward his basic ineptness in social situations.

The frustration of this need to avoid disapproval, which he used to experience, contributed to the development of aggression in him. But its contribution was less than the frustration of his need to gain approval. The sequence went like this: severe frustration of his need to gain approval plus mild frustration of his need to avoid disapproval led to a considerable need to aggress. The frustration of his need for approval ceased when he obtained a good job and a home. But he developed his disquieting habits as ways of venting the old aggression which remained and of avoiding the possibility of disapproval which also remained because of his awkward, uncertain personality.

Chapter 13

LAWBREAKERS

MUCH criminal behavior, particularly stealing, is directed toward attempting to satisfy both the need to aggress and the need to gain approval. It may seem a little farfetched to say crimes are committed partially for approval. However, most individuals who steal do so in order to "live high" and so gain the approval of their associates. Of course, known thieves bring a torrent of disapproval upon themselves from society in general. But most criminals do not expect to be caught. They are mainly concerned about the approval which they may gain from the people in their own antisocial groups; they want to be "big shots" in the eyes of their associates.

These same criminals have in the past been severely frustrated in their need for approval and the consequent need to aggress also usually motivates their criminal behavior. It is true that in some cases of violent crime the behavior is motivated only by aggressive feelings and is not directed toward gaining approval. This is the case when a man commits murder in a blind rage. He is obviously not trying to gain approval then. He is venting his aggression. However, the need to aggress generally will have arisen because the person whom he murders has caused, or been associated with, severe frustration of either his need for approval or his need to avoid disapproval.

The greater part of criminal behavior is motivated by both the needs to aggress and to gain approval. This is true in most instances of juvenile delinquency. Here is one instance when I was "fortunate" enough to see one of Madison's juvenile delinquents at close range. I had gotten up in the middle of the night and gone into the bathroom but hadn't turned on the light. As I came out

I heard scraping noises. I looked across the hall into the bedroom.

First, there was nothing. Then a dark shape appeared in the open bedroom window. It came through the window.

I stood stock still in the bathroom door. The shape moved to the bed, reached out and poked once. I reached behind the door and miraculously put my hand on a stick with a suction cup on the end.

The shape stood by the bed. I waited. Slowly, I pulled the rubber suction cup off the end of the stick. The shape started toward the bedroom door. I could see it clearly against the open window behind. I was sure it could see me. It came out in the hall, stopped right in front of me and waited. It turned left and I swung as hard as I could.

There was a short groan, the shape went down, and then there was complete silence.

I switched on the light. A boy of about seventeen was lying motionless on the hall floor with a gun near his hand. I picked up the gun and waited. The boy did not move. I got a chair and sat down beside him. I poked him with my toe and he moved. He groaned and put his hands to his head. Then he opened his eyes. I had the gun in my right hand and the stick in my left and I was sitting near him.

The boy looked as though his feelings were hurt more than his head. He touched his head and then he looked up at me. "What you do that for?" he said.

"What did I do that for!"

"I didn't think anybody was home," he said. He shook his head as if he couldn't understand it at all.

"We all make mistakes," I said. He was a smallish fellow and he didn't look very dangerous.

"I didn't think anybody was home," he said again.

He was dressed quite well in a flashy way—blue suit, pink shirt, loud tie, striped socks, and suede shoes. His hair was shiny. He started to get up, and I tapped him lightly on the head with the stick. He settled back on the floor and looked hurt. "That'll be enough of that," he said.

"What were you after?" I said.

"Now, what would I be after?" he said. "Me grandmother's eyeglasses maybe?"

He started to get up again and I pushed him in the chest with the stick. "Now don't get funny with me, fella," he said.

"How long have you been going into houses like this?"

"Since I was two."

"Now don't get funny with me, fella," I said.

"Three, four months," he said, quickly. Then he added, "I never been caught."

"Till now."

He didn't say anything.

"Don't you feel a little guilty about the idea of taking things other people might need?" I said.

"Oh, sure. Sure. It keeps me awake nights." Then he grinned. "But then, me work keeps me up at night, anyways."

"Suppose you took something someone really needed —money for food, for example. Wouldn't you feel bad?"

"Oh, sure. Like I told you—it'd keep me awake all night." He shook his head and laughed to himself. Then he looked at me and said, "Jesus, you're a lulu, you are."

"Seriously, wouldn't it bother you?"

"Why the hell should it?"

"Have you ever had a job?"

"Look," he said. "I gotta go now. I'll write you a letter."

I pushed him back down by jabbing the stick in his chest.

"Have you ever had a job?" I said.

"I don't work for no bastard for thirty bucks a week."

"You've never had a job?"

"I cleared a thousand since I been in business."

"In business?"

"Since I been operating."

"Oh."

"Now, look, fella," he said. "I gotta go. I gotta be on my way."

I waved the stick. "Where are your mother and father?"

"What the hell are you, one of them bug-doctors?"

"Where are they?"

"You must be nuts."

"Are they dead?"

"I don't know. Now, look, I—"

"Who brought you up?"

"I brought meself up. Look, I gotta go."

"You must be nuts," I said.

He studied me for a moment. "I gotta get home to the wife and kids. They'll be worried."

"Do you have a wife?"

"Oh, yeah. Three."

"Okay. You can get up," I said.

He got up and dusted off his blue suit with his hands. The jacket was very long.

"The gun," he said, and held out his hand. "Leave me have the gun."

"Let you have it?"

"That gun cost me." He looked straight at me. "Leave me have it. It ain't loaded anyways."

"You don't mind if I check," I said and moved back a step. It was loaded.

"It's loaded," I said.

"I didn't think it was."

"Sit down over there," I said.

He sat down and I called the police.

What causes boys like this to get started in crime? Almost invariably four things are true of their past environment. One, they have learned relatively high, if superficial, approval goals. For example, they may have learned that owning big sporty cars brings approval. Two, they have had little chance in school to begin preparation for an occupation which would make it possible for them to earn, in an acceptable way, the money to achieve their goals. Coming usually from lower-class families, they have been disapproved of in school and therefore have banded together into defensive little outgroups where the emphasis is on making the least, rather than the most, of education. Third, they have associated with individuals who have achieved, by criminal behavior, the same goals they desire. Four, they have been undersocialized—have not been approved of by their parents for behaving in ways which our society considers acceptable and disapproved of for behaving in ways considered unacceptable.

Because these boys have learned "high" goals for approval and because they know that they have little chance of ever earning the money to attain them, they feel frustrated. The frustration sets up in them the need to aggress. They feel hostile toward society in general because they feel society is purposely blocking them. They want to attain their goals and to aggress against society.

Then, if they come in contact with individuals who are achieving by unacceptable behavior the same goals they themselves want, they begin to imitate this behavior. Being undersocialized, they have not learned to feel any strong anxiety at the prospect of antisocial behavior. They learn habits such as stealing as ways of venting their hostility against society and as short cuts to the approval of their friends, who tend to be frustrated in much the same way as they are.

The boy who broke into my house did not bring himself up as he claims. His parents were poor but not poverty-stricken. They lived in a two-family house in Madison on the edge of Black Row. His mother had a job as a maid while he was growing up. His father worked off and on at whatever kind of work he could pick up. They let him do pretty much as he pleased. They were both undersocialized individuals themselves and they made little attempt to teach him acceptable ways of behavior.

When he was in grammar school, he became friends with a group of boys a few years older than he who lived in Black Row. To them, fancy clothes, a sporty car, and money to spend in bars and on girls were the things which stood for approval. There were a few still older fellows around Black Row who had attained these things through the simple process of stealing. The most successful of these was a flashy fellow named Duke Sheldon. He had a black mustache, a pink convertible, and a seemingly endless supply of pastel-colored suits and girl friends. He was a burglar but he always claimed, mock-seriously, to be a gambler. He was the idol of the group of boys with whom this boy who broke into my house became friends. They all wanted to be like him. The boy who broke into my house wanted to be like him, too. The boy was fifteen then. He wanted to be a big shot, like Duke Sheldon, but there was no chance of his ever earning the kind of money Duke threw around. Why shouldn't he relieve those who were so righteous of some of their easily earned money?

One Saturday night when he was sure no one was home the boy broke in a house in Fairview Manor and stole eighty-one dollars, a bottle of brandy, some silverware, and a wrist watch. Soon he was breaking into houses regularly. He vented his aggression against those who had what he did not have, he got the means to what stood for approval to him. He also gained the direct approval of his friends who began to think that he was really a big operator.

Go down to the Madison railroad station any weekday morning at 8:08 and you will be able to observe two men boarding the commuter's special. Both men are criminals and both commute to work. Regularly.

The tall well-dressed one steals fifteen thousand dollars annually—a little more in good years. The short, sloppy one steals anywhere from five thousand dollars a year in lean years to ten thousand in good years.

They do not know each other. Just by coincidence they sit down in the same seat this morning. The well-dressed man folds the morning paper with skill and begins to read. The other one slumps down in his seat and goes to sleep. Soon he begins to snore. The well-dressed man glances at him disdainfully and then turns back to his paper.

The short man is a pickpocket of considerable accomplishment. He roams the city from nine to five on the lookout for small crowds which have temporarily formed to watch something of interest.

The little man never circulates in large crowds. He never picks individuals who look wealthy nor does he pick the poor. He concentrates on the average type of person and tries to pick two pockets a day. He averages thirty dollars or so a day and is well pleased with himself. He takes pride in his skill and comfort in his moderation. He served a year in prison soon after he started in business as a young man. But that was for burglary. He has never been caught at picking pockets, and he is proud of his record.

The little man commutes because he is firmly convinced that this relieves him of any possibility of suspicion. Whenever he has to stay in town overnight he feels hunted, but as soon as he steps on the five-o'clock train for home he feels relaxed.

The other criminal operates somewhat differently. The tall man is a tax consultant. He specializes in tax evasion. He makes fifteen thousand and more a year advising fly-by-night companies how to cheat the government on taxes in ways which are not likely to be discovered. He gets a percentage of what he steals from the government.

He does not in any way feel that he is a criminal. Of course, he doesn't tell his friends in Madison that he specializes in tax evasion. They think of him as an accountant. He feels he is as honest as the next man and has nothing but contempt for any rascal who might remove fifteen dollars from someone else's cash register.

He is a self-made man and proud of it, too. He owns a ranch-type home in the Glenhaven section of Madison. Out on the back lawn there is a stone fireplace where on week ends, wearing a paper chef's cap, he broils steaks for his guests. His boy is the best student in the eighth grade and he hopes to send him to Harvard eventually. He wants to "give the boy something I never had." And then he reflects, "On the other hand, I've done pretty well without a high-class education. Main thing is hard work and common sense."

This gentleman and the pickpocket are both motivated by the need to aggress and the need for approval. In both cases their needs for approval have been frustrated in earlier years. Both were undersocialized and now they steal in order to gain the approval which money can buy and to aggress against the society which frustrated them.

The pickpocket is about fifty years old now. His name is Sam Gogel. When Sam was sixteen he was sent to this country from Europe. His parents had died and he was to live with an uncle here. He never saw the uncle, who had been in a little trouble with the law and fled to California. The boy shifted for himself, almost starving to death before he got a job at three dollars a week as an errand boy in a jewelry shop. The jeweler was of the same nationality as Sam and that was why Sam got the job. On three dollars a week he lived in a hall room and ate little more than bread. All around him in the city he saw what was to him unbelievable wealth.

Sam had no friends. There was no one to take the slightest interest in him. He saw boys his age having a carefree time. He wanted to be like them. He ached for approval. It seemed to him that the one thing which kept him from having friends, from being liked and admired, was his poverty.

In Europe, Sam's parents had been carnival people who had taught him little about the accepted ways of acting. In fact, his father's view had been to get what you could from the customers in whatever way you could. So the boy had no twinges of conscience when he began to speculate that everything would be different for him if some of the wealth of his employer were his.

Sam knew better than to steal from the shop. The jeweler kept a running inventory of every item. But the jeweler also kept a key to his home in a drawer of the desk in the back room of the shop. Sam had seen him give it to his wife once when she had misplaced her key. Sam waited his chance. Soon it came. One fine spring morning he overheard the jeweler telling a friend that he and his wife were going to a concert that evening. Just before closing time Sam took the key from the drawer of the desk.

That evening, from the doorway of a building across the street, he watched the jeweler and his wife leave their home for the concert. Then with no difficulty he removed from their home several pieces of jewelry and thirty-four dollars as well. The next morning Sam slipped the key back in the drawer of the desk in the back room of the shop. He went to the salesroom and began dusting the display cases. Suddenly the jeweler stood in front of him holding the key. Sam was terrified. He ran out of the shop. The police caught him and he spent over a year in prison. The jeweler had merely suspected him. Sam had given himself away, by running.

In prison Sam made friends for the first time since he had arrived in this country. One prisoner with whom he became particularly good friends was a pickpocket of high repute. The pickpocket was the leader of the group into which Sam was thrown and he enjoyed enormous prestige because of his professional abilities. His reputation did not seem to suffer in the least because his hand had slipped the last time it had been professionally utilized. This master pickpocket took the boy under his wing and during the long days taught him his art. Sam had never been a fast learner but he immediately grasped the practical aspect of the art and learned with amazing rapidity. Then too, it was fun.

Sam gained approval from both his teacher and the other prisoners; they were truly proud of him. "In five years, the kid'll have more class than I did at me peak," the master pickpocket used to say proudly.

On the other hand, the aggression developed by the frustration Sam had suffered before being convicted was aggravated by the physical confinement of prison. He began to think of everyone but the other prisoners as his enemy. By the time Sam left prison he was completely equipped for a life of antisocial endeavor: undersocialized, approval need frustrated, strong feelings of aggression, and a criminal skill, pocket-picking, for the learning of which he had received approval.

From the outset Sam was a success in his chosen field. He soon married a girl and they moved to Madison. Every day he commuted to his job—which his wife understood to be that of a salesman of wholesale costume jewelry.

Sam's wife, childless, died seven years ago. He still commutes regularly, though he has a total of twenty thousand dollars in six banks. He hasn't missed a day in twenty years. His need for approval has weakened since his wife's death: he lives simply and cares little what people think of him. But the strength of old habit and his continued feeling of aggression against society drive him to the city on the 8:08 Monday through Friday.

The behavior of the other commuter, the specialist in tax evasion, is motivated by both the need to aggress and the need for approval. Oddly enough, his parents tried their best to oversocialize him. At the same time, they gave him little warmth and affection. They were relatively old, being almost forty when he was born. They looked upon him as a miniature adult rather than as a growing, learning child. They expected him to do everything in exactly the right way from the start. But because little affection and little approval accompanied their insistence, he rebelled. Instead of becoming oversocialized he became undersocialized. He learned the opposite of what his parents, extremely frustrating individuals from his point of view, tried to make him learn.

His parents were people of fair means, and after he graduated from high school they insisted that he attend a business school. His father believed in "practical schooling" only and gave him his choice of an accounting course or a teachers' college. The boy wanted to go to a liberal arts college, since that was where his friends were going. His father would have none of that. The boy's only alternative to doing as his father wished was to take a low-paying job. He went to business school.

When he had finished the course, the only jobs available were what amounted to errand boy and junior clerk with accounting firms. He took such a job and hated it. His salary was so low that he had to live with his parents. They constantly nagged him for what they considered his lack of appreciation for their having sent him through "the finest accounting school in the state."

He would eventually have had a good career with the firm by which he was employed, but he was too impatient for that. He wanted to have money right away, to be someone people would take note of. He was not gaining any approval now and his parents had so frustrated him in earlier years that he was laden with pent-up aggression.

Then he fell in with a group of young accountants in the city who, as they said, "had it made." They lived in modern apartments, threw big parties, and dressed like executives. He was amazed. They were tax consultants and, as they told him, they "sold advice on how to cut your tax in half." Why didn't he go along with them? They didn't mind competition—it was a wide-open field. He was crazy if he didn't go along with them, they told him. He agreed with them. He was aware that their particular approach to their professional specialty was more than a shade illegal, but he had few scruples about such matters. The kind of approval their money brought was what he wanted. And as had been the case when he was a boy, it made him feel relaxed, less aggressive, just to think of taking a rebellious course of action: in this case that of advisor on how to cheat the government.

His new friends made the necessary contacts for him, and he was in business. He seemed to have a flair for tax evasion right from the start. In six months he moved into an apartment of his own. Soon he married a pretty, naive girl from Madison. After two years they had a child and decided to move out of the city to Madison. They bought a nice house in Glenhaven and have been there ever since. He calls himself D. Ross Hutchins now (he was born Donald R. Hutchins) and he is very happy taking the 8:08 to work every Monday through Friday morning. He is particularly happy on summer Saturday evenings wearing his paper chef's cap and broiling steaks for his friends while his son, who is going to go to Harvard, holds the plates ready.

Chapter 14

KILLERS

MURDER and suicide are but two variants of the same act—killing a human being. In either case, the need to aggress, occasioned by severe frustration, is usually one of the motivating forces. The murderer vents his aggression against another, the suicide against himself. As we shall see, a second driving force is the desire for satisfaction of the frustrated need itself—the need for approval or the need for avoiding disapproval.

Only one murder has been committed in Madison in recent years. That murder was committed on the thirteenth day of November in an old ornate house on Highland Avenue.

It was getting dark. The street lights had come on, but in the house there were no lights.

Downstairs in the big living room the woman said, "We'd better wait."

"We've waited long enough. Let's get it over with," the man said.

"She hasn't been so well," the woman said.

"Then why doesn't the old fool die?"

"Don't call her an old fool."

"Well, why the hell doesn't she? She's almost eighty-five," the man said.

"We'd better wait."

"We've been over it a hundred times. Let's get it over with."

"We'd better wait."

"Look. We agreed. Let's do it," he said.

"Suppose the fall doesn't kill her?" she said.

"It will."

"Maybe it won't."

"It will, I tell you."

"It might not. Then we'd have to kill her."

"Christ! We're killing her anyway."

"No. It's different if she falls."

"Let's do it now," the man said. "We go up to the

room and get her and start to help her down the stairs."

"She'll know," the woman said in the darkness.

"How? She can't even see."

"She'll know."

"Don't be so damned foolish. Come on."

"Suppose somebody finds out."

"They can't. No one can possibly find out. As soon as we're sure she's dead, we call Dr. Johnson and say we both were in the kitchen and heard her scream."

"You'll know," the woman said.

"Jesus Christ. We'll both know. You get on one side of her, I get on the other, like we always do. And then we both push together."

"It might not kill her."

"Of course it'll kill her. She's weak as a cat."

"If it doesn't you'll have to finish it."

"I'll finish it. Come on."

"I can't."

"What the hell do you mean you can't? Come on. She's not your mother. She's only an aunt."

"I know, but—"

"Two hundred thousand is a lot of money."

"I know."

"We'll probably have to wait ten years otherwise. And what for? It won't do her any good."

"No, it won't do her any good."

"Come on."

The man and the woman went up the stairs, along the hall and into a room.

Soon they came out of the room and moved toward the stairs.

"Get on the other side of her," the man said in the darkness.

"I am," the woman said. "You—"

"No. Together."

"You—"

"Come on. Now!"

There was a scream and heavy, bumping noises. Then, abruptly, the bumping noises stopped. There was dead silence.

"God damn it. You didn't push her," the man said.

"See—see if she's breathing."

"She's dead. Not a sound."

"See. I think she's alive," the woman said.

The man went down the stairs slowly.

"She's gone all right," he said.

"I feel sick," the woman said.

"Christ Almighty! You didn't even push her."

"Somebody will find out."

"Nobody will find out. Unless you—"

"Call Dr. Johnson."

"I'll call him now," the man said. . . .

The man's name is Henry Burton. The woman is his wife Catherine. The elderly lady whom they pushed down the stairs and killed was Catherine's aunt, Elizabeth Tryon. Elizabeth Tryon had what was left of the Tryon money—slightly over two hundred thousand dollars. She never married and, by the terms of her will, the money was to go to her niece.

But Henry and Catherine Burton are now in jail awaiting trial. A man named Homer Dunne was walking down Highland Avenue and heard the one scream. He did not think a great deal of it at the time but later he remembered and swore that he saw no lights in the house at the time of the scream. Henry and Catherine Burton had said they were in the kitchen with the light on, but some of the kitchen windows could be seen from the street.

It was Henry Burton's idea, not Catherine's, to murder Elizabeth Tryon. He persuaded his wife to agree. The older woman could not enjoy life any longer anyway, he told her. Catherine Burton is just as guilty as her husband but he was the instigator.

Henry Burton killed Elizabeth Tryon not for her money itself, of course, but for the approval which her money would bring. He and his wife were living in the old house on a small income. He wanted the approval which would come to him for living on a grander scale. Elizabeth Tryon had made it clear some years previously that she would not part with the Tryon money until her death. She was firmly convinced she would need large sums for medical care in the remaining years of her life. Besides, she did not like Henry Burton at all. She thought him a parasite, which he was. As she often said, he had never done an honest day's work in his life. In turn, he viewed her as his frustrator—which she was. Frustrated in his need for approval, he developed the need to aggress. Murdering Elizabeth Tryon, his frustrator, satisfied this need to aggress and well might have satisfied his need for approval—if he had turned the kitchen light on before pushing her down the stairs.

Henry Burton could satisfy his needs by murdering because he had a weak conscience. He never learned to feel the self-disapproval caused by the threat of severe disapproval by others which most people immediately feel when they consider committing some form or other of antisocial behavior.

Henry Burton's parents traveled extensively when he was young and left him in the charge of a nurse whom they thought was ideal but who completely neglected to teach him what is considered right and wrong in our society. She paid no attention to the child except to feed him and to discipline him when he annoyed her. As long as he did not annoy her, she did not care what he did.

Because of this upbringing, when Henry Burton considered killing Elizabeth Tryon, his needs to gain approval and to aggress were stronger than his self-disapproval at the thought of committing the act. So he killed her.

The part which Henry Burton's wife played in the murder was chiefly a passive one. She agreed to it, but with strong misgivings. In so agreeing, she was motivated in much the same way as her husband was but on a lesser scale. She wanted the money in order to satisfy her need for the approval of others but she did not want it as badly as her husband. She was frustrated by her aunt's previous refusal to part with the money. But she was not frustrated as greatly as her husband because her need for approval was not as strong as his. Therefore, her need for aggressive behavior was weaker than her husband's. However, Catherine Burton also wanted the approval of her husband. She loved him and was dependent on him emotionally. So when he proposed the murder, she, being somewhat undersocialized—although less so than he—agreed reluctantly to his plan.

Of course, the needs to aggress and to gain approval do not directly motivate all murder. Certain premeditated murders, committed for money, might conceivably involve only a need to gain the approval which that money could bring. On the other hand, some unpremeditated murders may involve only the need to aggress. In a moment of extreme frustration, the individual's need to aggress rises sharply and he may attempt to kill his frustrator. But in any case, whether murder be premeditated or not, whether both or only one of the needs to aggress and to gain approval are involved, it will always be true that the individual who commits murder is one who is basically undersocialized. He will not have learned the pangs of conscience, the inner anxiety, the internalization of social disapproval, which automatically guide most members of society away from antisocial behavior.

People in Madison keep saying, "Why on earth did he ever do it? Why would a man like that kill himself? He had everything to live for."

They are talking about John Caldwell, who ended his own life just two days ago.

John Caldwell was fifty-four. He was married to the former Elizabeth Bromfield, who came from a fine old Madison family. He is also survived by three children: a daughter who married a doctor, a son at Princeton, and a second daughter who just graduated from college and teaches at Miss Tooney's Country Day School.

John Caldwell lived in one of the smaller houses in Fairview Manor. He was a vice-president of the Madison Foam Rubber Company.

As people say, John Caldwell had never been sick a day in his life. What they mean is that he had never had any serious illness. But thinking back on it, people say that John Caldwell was, in one sense at least, a little unusual: he was—well—a little withdrawn. As the family doctor, Henry Hatfield, said, "John always gave you the feeling that he was on the outside of life —looking in."

The night before last, shortly after ten o'clock, John Caldwell put a bullet through the side of his head. He had been working up to this for most of his fifty-four years. By no means the main reason, but simply the straw that broke the camel's back, was the fact that he failed to attain the presidency of the Madison Foam Rubber Company. People in Madison dismiss this fact as completely irrelevant. "Why, John didn't want to be president. He was perfectly happy where he was."

Well, John Caldwell was not perfectly happy where he was. He did want to be president of Madison Foam

Rubber. Old George Whyte, president of Madison Foam Rubber, retired last month. There were three possibilities for the presidency: the president's son, George Whyte, Jr., a playboy if there ever was one; Tom Bartlett, the overworker; and John Caldwell. If George Whyte, Jr., had been made president, John Caldwell could have accepted this. He would have looked upon it as a political matter which was out of his hands.

However, Tom Bartlett got the presidency. Old G.W. would not trust his son with it. John Caldwell felt in competition with Tom Bartlett, who was fourteen years his junior. He felt he had failed when Bartlett was made president. In his heart, John Caldwell knew Bartlett was the man for the job. Bartlett was younger, more vigorous, and had more drive than he did. Over the years Bartlett would be able to do a better job for the company.

John Caldwell knew that he himself was a dependable vice-president, but Tom Bartlett's promotion brought home to him the fact that he never would go higher. It made John Caldwell feel, in his own terms, a failure, not only in business but in all respects. So he killed himself.

Why was this incident the straw that broke the camel's back? Why did Caldwell feel a failure in all respects in spite of having led a life which, objectively speaking, was far from that of a failure? Not one man out of ten thousand in John Caldwell's position would have killed himself. Why did Caldwell?

John Caldwell was a painfully oversocialized person. Superficially he appeared well adjusted. He had developed a calm and courtly manner. However, beneath that calm exterior, he had an exaggerated fear of disapproval. Over the years his need to avoid this fear was, in a rough and tumble world, necessarily frustrated again and again. These frustrations led to an ever-increasing mounting of aggression. His aggression could have no outlet. Caldwell was too highly oversocialized for that. He had no escape valve. The loss of the presidency of the Madison Foam Rubber Company to Tom Bartlett was a final frustration which made Caldwell feel worthless, disapproved, and which swelled his internal aggression to the bursting point.

In one stroke John Caldwell released his aggression

in the only way he could—against himself—and he avoided the fear of disapproval forever.

John Caldwell's father was a minister and very strict man. John's mother was a plain woman who lived by her husband's command. John was the only child. During the early years of his life, his maternal grandmother lived with the family. The family lived on a very small income.

John's father ruled the household, with the exception of the grandmother, with an iron hand. John's mother seemed to fear him; John did fear him. The father believed that iron discipline was the key to a good life. Many times, in his earliest years, John had to sleep on the floor because he had wet his bed. "Esther, put the rubber sheet on the floor under him so it won't leak down into the parlor," his father would say to his mother. "And roll up a blanket and lay it in front of the door so he won't get the draft."

Esther did her husband's bidding. John's grandmother reacted quite differently. "You must be out of your mind to put a little thing like that, that hardly knows this world, on the floor," she would say to John's father.

"That will be quite enough, Mrs. Canner," his father would reply.

John's grandmother was his friend, his only source of affection, and his defender during his early years. His mother was good to him in her way but she never could bring herself to question his father in any respect. The boy's grandmother was different. Invariably she would take his side with fierce determination. She did not sway his father but the boy knew she cared. And then too, she used to tell him fascinating stories of her early life on the frontier.

When John was five, his grandmother fell ill and three days later she died. When the boy realized that she was gone for good, he felt as if the world had dropped out from under him. He cried and screamed for hours. Then he began to writhe upon the floor, to kick the walls and to beat his head against them. The grandmother had been his only bulwark in a cruel world. He was greatly frustrated by his loss of her and was, in effect, trying to work off the aggression he felt.

"I will stop him," his father said. "It is unhealthy."

The father picked the hysterical boy up and carried

him upstairs. He whipped him with his belt. The whipping had the desired effect: after an initial increase of hysteria John did quiet down. He would not speak for days. His mother, doing what she thought best, told him repeatedly that he must never behave in such a terrible way again.

That happened forty-nine years ago. Since that time, John Caldwell never released his aggression outwardly. He was frustrated many times but he kept his aggression within himself. Once his rage was brought to a stand-still by his father's whipping of him, he began to feel that with his grandmother gone any action he might take against the frustrating world around him was completely hopeless. Before her death he had been a quiet child and now he became even more quiet. He did what he was told, no matter how frustrating, and he kept his aggression within himself. His father made the most of the situation and oversocialized the boy with all the strength of his convictions.

When John was twenty-two his father obtained a position for him with the Madison Foam Rubber Company, then named the Madison Rubber Company. George Whyte was his father's friend. As his father said, "You'd never do for the ministry. You might as well try to make some money."

John was a docile young man, but he was bright and well-mannered. He applied himself to his work and he was dependable. He rose steadily in the Madison Rubber Company.

Soon after John went to work for Madison Rubber his father died. A year later John married Elizabeth Bromfield. It was considered a very good marriage in Madison. Because of Elizabeth's family, his own family, and his position at the Madison Rubber Company John gradually attained a place of high prestige in the community.

But throughout his life John Caldwell was plagued by a feeling of inadequacy and helplessness. He never felt up to the job at hand at the Madison Rubber Company, although he always did a good job. Then, too, he always felt that he should be getting ahead faster. As the children were growing up he felt that he should be doing more for them, although he was doing all a man could do. The strong disapproving hand of his father was upon his shoulder throughout his life. It made John Caldwell disapprove of himself no matter what he did.

His self-disapproval led to frustration and anxiety. As a result, he had strong aggressive feelings. They were repressed as quickly as they developed, because of his father's influence. A feeling of helplessness to rid himself of those feelings of aggression was always with him.

Obviously, not all cases of suicide involve a domineering father such as John Caldwell's. But in most cases, the individual will have been severely oversocialized as a child. Also, he will generally have experienced some extraordinarily severe frustration in early life, often the loss of someone who loved him greatly. He will generally have been harshly punished for quite naturally venting the aggression caused by this severe frustration. Feeling any outward release of aggression to be a futile effort, he will accept the strict demands of one or both of his parents and develop into a painfully oversocialized youth and adult. He will disapprove of himself no matter what his action and he will repress all consequent feelings of aggression. Then, if there arises a situation or a series of situations which to him spell particularly extreme disapproval and therefore extreme frustration and aggression, he is put in a position where suicide seems the only way out.

Chapter 15

HUMOROUS AND OTHERWISE

THE HUMOROUS and the would-be humorous abound in Madison as elsewhere. I was about to describe a humorous fellow of my acquaintance named Snooky Barnett. However, on thinking it over, I'm not so sure he's funny. Snooky is always asking, "Have you heard the one about the bridegroom who got caught in the rain?" Or "Have you heard the one about the Swedish girl who ran out of gas?"

Everyone always answers, "No, I don't believe I've heard that one," and then Snooky says, "Well, I have and it's not very good so I won't bother to tell it."

I guess we'll just forget about Snooky.

We all know people who are humorous. But what makes them so? First of all, humor is learned as are practically all other patterns of behavior. People learn the habit of being humorous as a way of satisfying one or more of their needs for approval, for avoiding disapproval, and for aggression. If a person happens to say or do something which makes others laugh, then they will approve of him. And so he repeats the behavior, presumably with variations, so that he will gain more approval.

People may attempt to be humorous in order to avoid disapproval or the threat of it when they get in a situation which promises to be a bit embarrassing. A man is unexpectedly called upon at a dinner to make a little speech, let us say. Immediately he is afraid of making a fool of himself. So what does he do? He dredges his memory and comes up with an old joke. He prefaces his telling of the joke by saying that he was reminded of it by such and such as he was driving over to the dinner. He tells the joke, everyone laughs a little, and he has the feeling that there is no longer a threat of disapproval. So then he says that happens to remind him of another joke.

He tells the second joke and then he sits down, having gotten around the speech nicely. He is relieved and so is everyone else. If the jokes have not been too bad he has probably managed to avoid the disapproval that would have come from making a bumbling speech.

The humorous person often releases aggression by his behavior. For example, the fellow who is always talking about how it will only be sensible for him to marry for money after his wife falls down the cellar stairs for the last time is venting a little aggression against his beloved spouse. This is not to say that he consciously hates his wife and has strong feelings of aggression toward her. But in the course of everyday living he and his wife are bound to frustrate each other a bit and therefore build up some aggression. A little humor is a most acceptable way of dispelling that aggression. It is probably better to josh about marrying for money after the little woman falls down the stairs than to bring about that most unfortunate end by giving her a little nudge.

When this fellow joshes about this matter, his wife will probably smile weakly as if to say, "Charlie's a great kidder." The other wives in the crowd will be, let us say, a trifle reserved in their appreciation of Charlie's little joke. But the husbands will think old Charlie is a howl. This gives them a chance to release, indirectly, a little aggression against their own spouses. Charlie feels better; he vents a bit of aggression and he gets a little approval from the other males in the crowd. The other males feel better; they release a little aggression, thanks to good old Charlie. And the ladies—well they have their little jokes, too.

This brings up the question of what needs humor satisfies for those who see and hear it. As in the case of Charlie's male friends, the humorous situation often provides an opportunity to release aggression vicariously and acceptably. Release of aggression reduces tension. This may be the case when one sees a practical joke played, such as a fellow getting a hotfoot or smoking an exploding cigar, or when one sees the inevitable cartoon of the explorers peeking out of the cannibals' big cooking pots. Likewise it may be the case when one sees the cartoons of men with butterfly nets suddenly being chased by gigantic, man-devouring butterflies; or the eerie cartoons where little boys go earnestly and happily about the business of setting dynamite charges under school buildings and the like.

When we see these practical jokes played and when we see these cartoons we are able to vent vicariously our aggressions against a society which has always prevented us from doing many things we would really like to do. When we were children, parents and teachers usually punished us, and frustrated our needs, when we did things considered unacceptable and aggressive. As adults, society holds over us the threat of disapproval or even of physical punishment to keep us from doing many things we'd like to do. Much humor gives us a chance vicariously to do these things—to stick out our tongues at that society which has frustrated us or threatened to frustrate us.

A second function of humor is that it boosts our feelings of approval and diminishes our feelings of disapproval. This is often the case with jokes, cartoons, and situations where someone is the goat or fool. There are always people who find hilarious any joke in which there is a character who stutters or lisps. It makes them feel momentarily superior and so relaxes them. You can usually get a laugh when you tell about the time that you made a slight mistake in a restaurant, about which door said "Ladies" and which said "Gentlemen."

Here are four other patterns of behavior, all less acceptable than humor, which people sometimes learn in their efforts to gain approval, avoid disapproval, and vent aggression at the same time. The first is petty officiousness. You can find this practically anywhere without looking too hard. But for the sake of convenience, let's take a look in the Madison branch office of the state motor vehicle department.

The clerk scratches her head. This is a problem of great dimensions. You want to apply for a driver's license, but you already have an out-of-state driving license.

She stops chewing her gum and an expression of faint disgust appears on her face. "If it was Massachusetts you come from, I'd know what to do," she announces through the bars of the application window.

The lady gives the matter further study and then calls out, "Mr. Ames, do you—"

"Yes, what is it?" replies a crisp voice from behind her.

Suddenly a sharp-nosed head with dark green reading visor tied on pokes into view. "Yes. Yes. What is it?" says Mr. Ames.

"This guy's got an out-of-state license and he wants—"

"Give it here," Ames says tersely.

She gives it there and waits, chewing slowly.

Ames adjusts his glasses under the green visor and then holds the license up for close scrutiny. He purses his lips. "I'll handle this personal," he says.

The lady sighs and sinks onto a stool.

Ames inspects the license at length, inspects you briefly, and then inspects the license at further length.

Finally, he points to your name on the license with his pencil, "That your name?" he asks, watching your every move.

"Yes."

Ames thinks behind his green visor and then, suddenly, makes his decision. "All right. Answer this," he snaps, sliding a long printed form toward you with an expert flip of his wrist. It is the written examination for a driver's license. There is no road test if you have a license from another state.

You begin to fill in the top of the form. "Not there," barks Ames. You look up at him and he jerks his head toward the wall to your far right. The form is supposed to be filled out at the desk over there and not at the application window. You take the form over to the wall desk. Ames goes back to matters of importance without showing the slightest strain of responsibility in the face of his position both as the governor's official representative for dealing with the driving public and as commander of branch office Number Twenty-seven.

You make a guess as to whether an automobile rear light must be visible for 100, 200, 300, or 325 feet on a foggy night going thirty miles an hour around a sharp curve. How many feet does it take to stop when traveling too fast? You decide not to write in "just one" and carry on to matters of finger-pointing on a right turn.

The examination filled out, you take it back to the

application window. The lady looks at you from her stool. Clearly it is no longer her problem. Ames sees you out of the corner of his eye but continues to stamp official documents.

"Here's the examination," you say, loud enough so he can hear you.

Ames looks over at you, returns his eyes to the business at hand, stamps two more official documents, sets his stamp down carefully, gets up and comes to the window. He picks up the examination, appraises it quickly, and says, "In ink."

He walks away, turns and says, "You see the pens and ink over there, don't you?" He shakes his head and returns to official business. It does not say on the examination that it should be filled out in ink, but it is probably true that you should have reasoned ink was necessary.

You scratch over your pencil marks with the official pen, try to wipe the ink off the fingers and return to the window.

"Here it is," you say.

Eventually Ames approaches the window. He picks up the form, looks at it closely. He takes out a card with the answers on it, lines it up alongside the form, and starts to correct your answers. You watch.

No mistakes so far.

Two thirds of the way down, Ames suddenly makes a red slash on the paper with his pencil. He smiles, shakes his head and goes on. He finishes, brushes the form aside and expertly slides you a small, square white card. He strides to the eye chart, points to line three and says, "Read that with your left eye covered."

You can hardly see the chart through the bars and at the extreme angle.

"Over there," Ames growls. There is a position over at the left end of the counter from which you are supposed to view the chart. You walk over to it and cover your eye with the card.

"I said left eye," Ames says slowly and with great self-control.

You have covered the wrong eye.

Ames drops his arm from the chart and stands, both arms hanging, "Look, mister, I don't have all day."

You read line three. You read the other lines—on command—backwards, forwards, left eye, right eye.

Ames picks up a book and flips the cover open. It is the color-blindness test showing close green spots like dried peas and orange curved numbers popping out at you. He flips the pages and you name the numbers fast.

Ames flips faster. You are running out of breath. He comes to the end, snaps the book closed, and strides back to the window.

"Fill that out," he says, and slides a green application form toward you. "All of it," he adds.

You fill it out in ink and take it back to him. From under his green visor, Ames gives it a quick glance and says, "It says to give middle initial, not middle name. Don't you read well, mister?"

The lady snickers from the stool.

You look at the form. Ames is right, of course.

Finally everything is acceptable to Ames. He states the fee. You give him a twenty-dollar bill.

"We don't run a bank here," he says, sharp nose quivering, and draws back the license. He watches to see what you'll do next.

"I'll go and get it changed," you say.

"That's your problem, mister," Ames says. He turns, goes back to his official documents, adjusts his green visor, and takes up his rubber stamp.

You get the bill changed down the street and return to your government's branch office for motor vehicles.

At the far end of the part of the room on the other side of the counter, Ames is speaking sharply to a young male clerk with narrow shoulders. "You young fellows are all alike," Ames says. "You think the world owes you a living without you moving a finger. Now, you file them proper from now on or you'll soon find out different."

Ames turns from the young clerk and sees you at the window. He counts your money deliberately and loudly. Then he looks straight at you, shakes his head, flips the license across the counter, and walks away.

As you open the door to leave, Ames nods toward you and says to the lady who is still upon the stool, "Jesus, they're something, ain't they?"

"Yeah, ain't they, though?" replies the lady on the stool.

What makes brother Ames so disagreeable, so snappish, so given to petty officiousness? Obviously, there is quite a lot of aggression behind that green visor. And it is clear that he craves importance.

Ames has held that same small job as chief of the Madison branch office of the state motor vehicle department for eighteen years. He is not particularly intelligent and he does not have the ability to hold a job with more responsibility, but he has never realized that. He wishes to be a man of importance—State Commissioner of Motor Vehicles would do nicely. He knows now that he never will be and so he feels frustrated.

The situation is not improved any by Mrs. Ames, a nagging, bossing wife if there ever was one. That lady brings to her spouse's attention with daily regularity his failure to achieve a position of high income and prestige. As she explains to him, "You're nothing but a jellyfish." And then, inevitably, she reminds him, "I should have married Billy Porges when I had the chance. Things would have been different then, all right." William Porges was a rising purveyor of fresh applejack in the late 1920's and is now sole owner of the highly successful Pink Elephant night club.

Mrs. Ames only intensifies Ames' feeling of frustration at having failed to become a man of importance. But Ames is a fairly well-socialized individual and he does not vent his aggression by either clipping Mrs. Ames about the chops or becoming physically aggressive toward other members of the community. Instead, he vents his aggression in a somewhat veiled way on the applicants for licenses and registrations who come into the motor vehicle office and on the young male clerk who works under him. He snaps at the applicants and derides them for failing to fill out forms correctly, although there is no particular reason why they should know how to. He browbeats the young clerk unmercifully.

In doing these things Ames is not only trying to release some of the aggression he feels because of his own failure to gain a position of importance. He is also trying to gain approval and avoid disapproval by his actions. He wants people to take notice of him as a man of strength and responsibility who will stand for no nonsense. At the same time, his behavior is a defense by which he tries to throw attention away from his true lack of importance.

Underneath Ames' rather obnoxious exterior, there dwells a rather nice fellow who feels he is a failure and who simply wants people to think well of him. But the habits he has developed over the years for trying to release aggression, gain approval, and avoid disapproval are ones which only lead people to disapprove of him. Being in a position of petty authority, he does not realize this. The young clerk who works under him does not dare indicate disapproval of him. People who apply for licenses and car registrations are usually too anxious about not passing the test or not filling out the forms correctly to make an issue of Ames' aggressive impoliteness and officiousness.

Incidentally, the lady clerk who works under Ames is the one person other than his wife upon whom he does not vent his aggression. She has the key to Ames' personality. She simply tells him frequently, but in varied ways, what an extremely responsible position he holds, how hard he works, and how intelligent he is.

On first meeting him, you'd never think Oscar Roberts was a race hater. Oscar was born in the hills of Tennessee. He has been out of the hills for twelve years now, since he was eighteen, but he is still very shy and quiet except on certain occasions.

I knew Oscar during the war and when he was north on a business trip last year he looked me up.

"How are things, Oscar?" I asked him.

"Right fine. Right fine," he said. Oscar sounds very sincere.

After we had refought the war rather thoroughly, I said, "Would you like me to show you around town, Oscar?"

"Let's jest drive around a bit," Oscar said.

We drove around and he remarked on how nice everything was. Oscar is very soft-spoken and uses the word "nice" a great deal.

We came to the rotary circle downtown and started around it. A car from the right cut in front of us going fast and I slammed on the brakes.

"Git him!" Oscar yelled. "Git him!"

"Git who?" I said. I couldn't figure out what had come over the mild Oscar. He was red in the face.

"Why that black son of a bitch. Git him!"

Then I realized that the driver of the car which cut across in front of us had been a Negro.

"Everybody cuts in front of you around here," I said.

"Don't make no matter," Oscar said. "Why that black son of a bitch ought to be tarred and feathered."

I thought the mild Oscar was going to have a stroke.

"I didn't know you felt that way about Negroes, Oscar," I said.

"If that'd been down home, we'd a caught that fellow and drug him out of his car and taught him a lesson he wouldn't forgit for some time."

"Well, whites cut in front of you all the time, too."

"Them black bastards shouldn't be given drivin' licenses anyway," Oscar said. "Ought to be kept where they belong."

"Where is that?"

"Where they belong. They ain't as good as animals," Oscar answered.

"That's the park over there," I said. There were swans on the little lake.

"That's mighty nice," the mild Oscar said. Then he muttered, "That black bastard."

Prejudice toward Negroes or any other group is primarily a way of venting aggression which has resulted from frustration of the race hater's own need for approval. In certain groups where racial prejudice is a part of the group's subculture it is a fully acceptable way of releasing aggression and sometimes is, in fact, a required way. If you are white and live in certain sections of the South, you are suspect if you do not profess to hate Negroes.

Thus, racial prejudice is also directed toward attempting to gain approval and avoid disapproval. If one is a member of a racially prejudiced group or community, one actually does gain approval and prestige from the rest of the group or community if he establishes himself as a fearless fighter for "white supremacy." Besides, if he can degrade another group, he may succeed in drawing attention away from the shortcomings of his own group and himself and thereby avoid the disapproval of others. Even if he does not succeed in avoiding the disapproval of those outside his own prejudiced group, he will in all probability succeed in convincing himself and those in his group that he and they are, by contrast with those against whom the prejudice is directed, men of rare distinction.

You will note that the most extreme and violent race haters are often individuals who are themselves most frustrated in their attempts to gain approval. For example, in parts of the South the white sharecroppers, who lack prestige almost as much as the Negroes, are often the most violently anti-Negro. They are frustrated more than the other whites, therefore feel more aggressive. In their communities, racial prejudice is a fully acceptable way of ridding themselves of that aggression.

People tend to learn racial prejudice if it is a part of their subculture. Parents pass it on to children through what amounts to informal teaching. In prejudiced groups, race hating is a part of the process of socializing the child. In effect, he gains approval for learning it and disapproval for not learning it. For people like Oscar Roberts, learning attitudes of racial prejudice is natural. Prejudice, once learned, thrives heartily because it gives the individual an outlet for his aggression, often nets him approval, and sometimes succeeds in drawing attention away from his own shortcomings.

The fellow who is always jealous about his wife, who unjustly suspects her of paying too much attention to other men and then raises hell with her about it, is another type whose behavior falls within this broad category of people who try to vent aggression, gain approval, and avoid disapproval—all at the same time.

Phil Angelo, owner of a small contracting business in Madison, is a jealous husband. Phil and his wife live in the Breezy Acres development. They have a number of friends living close by, and every Saturday night they all get together at one house or another "for a few laughs." Lately Phil has been a little short on laughs.

Two Saturday nights ago, everyone was at the Browns'—who live across the street from the Angelos—just for a few laughs.

Halfway through the evening, Phil's wife, Agnes, left the Browns' living room and went along the hall to the bedroom where the ladies had left their coats on the bed. She found her handbag, sat down at the dressing table, and took out her powder and lipstick. She started to apply them and then, not quite knowing why, turned and glanced behind her.

Phil was standing just inside the doorway, with his arms folded. "I hope you're enjoying yourself," he said.

"What?"

"I said I hope you're enjoying yourself." Phil stood looking at her. "But then it's easy to see you are."

"Oh, Phil. Don't tell me you're going to start that again. For heaven's sakes, when will you—"

Phil put up his hand. "That will do. Just what the hell have you and Ben Martin been doing over in the corner for the last half-hour? Do you think I'm blind?"

"Phil—"

"What's he got that pencil and paper in his hand for? What's he doing, turning psychiatrist?"

"I was just giving him the recipe for that veal dish I make." Agnes spoke each word slowly and very distinctly. "We were over in the corner because that's where the desk is, and Ben needed a pencil and paper to take down the recipe."

"That's a rich one, that is. Since when did Ben—"

"You know Ben likes to cook."

"I always thought he was a little queer, if that's what you mean."

"Phil, will you please believe me when I tell you I'm only trying to be pleasant to other people. Now let's go back. It looks odd for us to be in here."

"What's the matter? Can't you wait to dance with Matthews again?"

Agnes spoke slowly and distinctly again. "He asked me to dance. What should I do, say 'How dare you?'"

"Break it up, you two." It was Helen Simmons coming in to get her handbag. "You're just like a couple of newlyweds, going off together like this."

"Hi, Helen," Agnes said.

"Hi, Helen, how's tricks?" Phil said.

Phil goes on like this every time he and his wife get together with their friends. The truth is that Agnes does not have any undue interest in other men. She merely tries to be polite and pleasant, with both men and women alike. But Phil misinterprets her actions for a number of reasons.

Primarily, he does so in order to avoid the threat of

disapproval. Because his parents were undependable people who rewarded and punished him without any logical consistency, he has learned to feel that people in general are undependable. Thus he feels insecure about his wife and is genuinely afraid that she might become attracted to another man. He feels that if she were to do so he would look an awful fool and be laughed at by his friends. The possibility of this is so real to him that the threat of it alone causes him much anxiety and frustration. So he tries, by his nagging behavior, to forestall the possibility of his wife's becoming attracted to another man.

Phil himself has fleeting thoughts of infidelity now and then, as do many people. Being fairly well socialized, he feels guilty about those thoughts, feels anxious about the disapproval they would bring him if people knew them. By being jealous of his wife and accusing her of undue interest in other men, Phil is unconsciously projecting his own thoughts of infidelity onto her. In so doing he is attempting to reduce his guilt feelings.

Apart from feeling a frustration of his need to avoid disapproval, Phil also feels a frustration of his need to gain approval. By his jealous behavior he is trying to increase the amount of attention, affection, and approval which his wife gives him. He tries to force her into a position where she will feel it necessary to give him more attention. She gives him a normal amount but he feels that she does not. He sees her listening and paying attention to other men in what are actually polite, accepted ways. But he thinks that this attention should go to him. He does not realize that if she were to direct her attention toward him only, other people would think her an antisocial person.

Now, these frustrations of Phil's needs for avoiding disapproval and gaining approval seem imaginary to us, but they are real to him. As a result, he has developed a considerable amount of aggression within him. Phil's jealousy is also a way of releasing a significant portion of that aggression, as well as of trying to avoid disapproval and to gain approval. He hurts his wife by his insinuations and accusations and he unconsciously knows that. In fact, his behavior is more effective in providing an outlet for his aggression than it is in enabling him to avoid disapproval or gain approval.

Last in this group we have the bombastic type—the fellow who seems to think that fierce loudness marks him as a man of stature. P. Armstrong Worth IV is such a man. P. Armstrong is the president of the largest company (Worth-More Products) in the vicinity of Madison and he lets you know it. He is big and he is loud. He is also a snap-decision man.

P. Armstrong holds business conferences almost daily. The procedure is this: P. Armstrong sits in a big leather chair well back from one end of the long table. His aides sit around the table on straight-backed chairs. They present, in turn, their information on the problem at hand. P. Armstrong bellows their names and they report. It is like a parade ground with sitting troops.

"Morris!" booms P. Armstrong.

Morris, a lean, precise fellow, reports incisively and then retreats, figuratively, two paces.

"Jones!" P. Armstrong bellows and a slight smile curls along his upper lip, tilting the bristly mustache. Jones is a bright young man but he has a habit of speaking haltingly, of seeming to fumble for his words. Now, as he speaks, he almost stutters.

"To the point, man! To the point!" P. Armstrong snarls.

Jones wavers, then goes on. As he reaches the end of his report he picks up speed and seems to fall across the finish line, completely exhausted. He caves back in his chair.

"Son of a bitch," says P. Armstrong of Jones' endeavors. P. Armstrong swings his massive jaw toward Jones and curls his upper lip.

Jones studies the papers in front of him.

"Warren!" booms P. Armstrong finally.

Warren begins to speak and P. Armstrong interrupts him: "And for Christ's sakes, spit it out!"

Warren spits it out accurately and perhaps a bit too rapidly.

He finishes and P. Armstrong says, "Don't try to be a God-damned tobacco auctioneer, Warren."

The remaining staff members report on command.

After the last report is in, there is silence while The General considers. (P. Armstrong's staff call him The General, not to his face, but only when he can overhear them.)

The problem at hand concerns whether or not to replace the old machinery in Section 4 of the Worth-More plant. General Armstrong slowly swings his massive jaw from left to right. Against the backdrop of his aides' silence, he says, "Son of a bitch," clearly, with nice pauses between the words. He is considering.

Suddenly he lunges from his chair, bellows "Do it!"—and marches from the conference room.

As the door slams behind him, not many are aware that P. Armstrong's bombast is a cover-up for his insecurity, for a fear of disapproval. It is also a workable way of letting off aggression and of gaining a kind of grudging approval from his business associates.

But is it really possible that a man among men like P. Armstrong is afraid of disapproval? After all, he is a success: he is rich, president of a company, and his wife drives a white Jaguar.

P. Armstrong's family was wealthy. His father, P. Armstrong Worth III, was president of the company and as domineering as they come. As he always said, from somewhere between his collar and his thick mustache, "There is a time and a place for everything," and he had nothing against babies crying as long as they confined it to the period between nine in the morning and five in the afternoon—weekdays only. P. Armstrong III disapproved loudly of his young heir, P. Armstrong Worth IV—and everyone else—upon the slightest provocation.

When P. Armstrong IV went away to school at age fourteen, he was a quiet, somewhat shy lad. The other boys immediately started to take advantage of him. But P. Armstrong was large for his age then, even as he is now. He was forced into a number of fights and he won easily. He soon found that if he asserted himself, spoke out loudly and threatened to fight anyone who tried to intimidate him, he was respected for it. He still felt unsure of himself but the groundwork for his bombastic ways was being firmly laid.

P. Armstrong III died of a heart attack only a few years after P. Armstrong IV graduated from college. The elder Worth had been strong in his desire to have the leadership of Worth-More Products remain within the family. Thus it fell to the fourth P. Armstrong to take over the reins of the company, young as he was.

He felt extremely anxious about doing so. He had little real confidence in himself, but he knew that if he displayed weakness, the vice-presidents would walk over him from that time forward.

On his first day as president of Worth-More Products, P. Armstrong called a meeting of the staff. He knew he had complete authority and that helped him to steel himself for what he was about to do. He gave no one a chance to speak. He took the bull by the horns and began to rave about how badly things had been going downhill since his father's illness. He wasn't really sure whether the company had been going downhill or uphill or any other way, but he acted as if he were sure.

Fortunately he was right. The company had been going downhill for some years prior to his father's illness. In his later years, his father had been reluctant to make necessary changes in the plant and as a result production had been hurt. The vice-presidents were relieved to see that some action was apparently about to be taken. But P. Armstrong had no way of knowing that that was their reaction. When he finished his speech he walked out of the conference room, shaking within himself. He was afraid he had gone too far.

Late that afternoon old Bill Donahue, the senior vice-president, came to P. Armstrong's office and said, "I just want you to know we're all behind you, son."

P. Armstrong knew then that he had made the right move and he knew enough to follow it up. "Donahue, you tell them they'd damn well better be, or there'll be somebody else behind me," P. Armstrong said.

Then he went over and put his hand on old Bill Donahue's shoulder. "One other thing. I don't care what you call me when we're at the club, but in this plant don't call me son."

Over the years P. Armstrong's bombast has become second nature to him. It solved the problem for him in school, it solved the problem when he took over the company, and it has worked ever since. P. Armstrong still has a vague feeling of threatening disapproval with respect to any action he is about to take. But the feeling is banished the moment he begins to shout. His shouting and bellowing give him confidence; he feels people look up to him rather than disapprove of him. In a sense, he is right. They do respect him for it, in a way. "P.A. is a mean cuss but, by God, he gets things done," they say. "You've got to hand it to him."

After all, aggression of P. Armstrong's type is a more or less accepted behavior pattern of the business subculture in which he operates. In a secret, half-conscious way many men would like to recast themselves in the mold of P. Armstrong. For not only does his behavior enable him to avoid feelings of disapproval and to gain a kind of approval; it is also an efficient way of satisfying that need to aggress, arising from the inevitable frustrations of life, which all men have.

PART V

AGGRESSION

Wife Beater: He'd come to see his wife as the cause of his failure . . .

IN SOME CASES, individuals who are frustrated in their need for approval or for avoiding disapproval (and who therefore have a need to aggress) temporarily direct their behavior toward trying to satisfy only their need to aggress. In these cases, the individual's behavior may lead to traces of satisfaction of his need for approval—either through self-approval or the approval of some individuals in his social environment. But in the main he is concerned, at the given time, only with the satisfaction of his need to aggress.

Chapter 16

EXTREMISTS

SOME PEOPLE go to rather unacceptable extremes in venting their aggression. Rape and sadism are two examples of such extremes.

The young man was in a cell in the Madison jail waiting to be taken to the state prison. He was charged with rape and had already admitted it. The girl he had raped the night before was in the Madison hospital in a state of shock.

The policeman walked down the corridor between the cells ticking his night stick lightly against the bars as he went. His blue-black shirt was tight and shiny over his big belly. He stopped in front of the cell the young man was in. The policeman had just finished breakfast and now he belched. The young man did not look toward him. The policeman reached in between the bars of the cell with his night stick and poked the young man in the ribs. The young man swung around and grabbed for the stick but the policeman easily pulled it back through the bars.

The policeman laughed. Then he took out a cigar, inspected it, rolled it around on his tongue, put it in his mouth and lighted it. "How's it goin', lover?" he said.

The young man did not answer him.

"Too bad," the policeman said. "Too bad. I really feel for you."

"Why don't you mind your own goddam business?" the young man said.

"How could you *do* such a thing?" the policeman said, making his voice sound effeminate.

"I'd do it again, if I had the chance," the young man said, looking at the policeman now.

"They're gonna burn you," the policeman said.

The young man did not answer.

"I hear the girl died," the policeman said, flicking the ash off his cigar with the little finger.

"I don't give a goddam if she did."

The policeman puffed on his cigar and put his big red face up close to the bars. "How was it, kid?" he said. "How was it?"

"Why don't you try it sometime?" the young man said. One of his front teeth was missing.

"Nah, I wouldn't like to fry," the policeman said.

He put his right hand, which was holding the night stick, up along one bar above his head. He watched the young man closely. "You, you're gonna fry. They're gonna fry you to a nice brown crisp."

The young man grabbed for him through the bars. The policeman brought the night stick down on the young man's head and stepped back. The young man clapped his hands to his head. The policeman laughed and went on down the corridor.

The young man's head ached sharply but it had ached before the policeman had come. That goddam son of a bitch, he said to himself, over and over.

Jesus, I've really had it, the young man thought. I'll be in jail the rest of my life. Maybe they *will* kill me. No, they can't. Why the hell did I ever do such a crazy thing? I just seen her and pulled out the knife and done it. She can't have died. No, she couldn't have. But I musta scared hell out of her. Maybe she was a nice kid. No, she's a bitch like all of them.

The policeman came back along the corridor, clicking his night stick against the bars as he came. He stopped in front of the cell the young man was in. He puffed on his cigar. "Why don't you pray, kid?" he said. "Might be it would keep you from fryin' down below—although I doubt that it would keep you from fryin' up here." He took the cigar out of his mouth and laughed.

The young man tried to hold himself together.

The policeman puffed on his cigar, took it out of his mouth again and flipped it through the bars. "Smoke, kid?" he said. The cigar hit the young man behind the ear and dropped to the floor, scattering ashes.

The young man grabbed it and threw it at the policeman in one motion. "You goddam son of a bitch," he said.

"Don't smoke, kid?" the policeman said. "Just as well. Just as well. Gives you cancer nowadays, you know. Oh, I forgot, cancer wouldn't bother you though, seein' as how you're gonna fry, anyways." He laughed and went on along the corridor, ticking his night stick lightly against the bars.

That son of a bitch must be nuts, the young man thought. But Christ, maybe he's right. Maybe I will get the chair. No, I can't though. I would if she died. She can't be dead though. She couldn't die. I didn't hurt her. It seemed like at the time I couldn't help it. I coulda gone to a whore house and had a hell of a sight better time. It wasn't that. I don't know. I couldn't help it. I never done it before. But Jesus, I've had it now....

First we will try to see why this young man, whose name is Frank, committed rape. Then we will look at the policeman, a sadist of sorts, and try to see what makes him tick.

As the young man, Frank, realized, he "could have gone to a whore house." He could have satisfied his need for sexual outlet by other means than rape. Every rapist has learned behavior other than rape for satisfying that need. But the need for sexual outlet is neither the only nor the most important need behind rape. It is necessary that the need for sexual outlet be present, of course. Given that, however, rape behavior is really an attempt to satisfy another need.

The real need that this boy Frank was trying to satisfy by raping a girl was the need to aggress. This is the primary need behind most rape behavior. Most rapists are, like Frank, starved for approval and hurt by disapproval. As a consequence they develop strong feelings of aggression. They tend to be very undersocialized and so their aggression is released against society in an unacceptable way.

But why does the aggression take the specific form of rape? It does so because they see women as the main frustrators of their needs for approval and for avoiding disapproval. And they unconsciously choose rape as the most satisfying way of aggressing against their frustrators because of the humiliation it causes. Potential rapists often belong to gangs whose members also feel aggressive toward women. They approve of rape as a way of humiliating women and raising their own self-esteem.

Frank was born and grew up in Madison's most rundown section—Black Row. His mother did not like the idea of having her freedom cramped by a child. When Frank was three years old, she frequently went off for most of the day and left him alone in the tenement apartment. She never bothered to teach him the socially accepted ways of gaining approval and avoiding disapproval. Even if she had bothered, it would have done little good for she herself did not know what the accepted ways were.

When Frank was seven, his mother left his father and went off with another man. Frank's father didn't much care about that, or about Frank, or about anything else but liquor. He worked occasionally as a furniture mover's assistant. Many a small item of furniture disappeared when he was on the job, and with the money he made he could enjoy the drinks and good fellowship of the Gaiety Bar and Grill.

Frank shifted for himself. He was always rather dirty and the teachers in the early grades of school scolded him for it and drew attention to it. He grew up hating everyone except the other white boys who lived in Black Row.

From his early teens on, Frank was a member of a gang of boys who called themselves "The Spikes." They liked the tough sound of the name. They called each other Spike, particularly when other people were around.

They were all boys whom the people of Madison looked down on individually. So they banded together in unconscious defense and hated the people of Madison in return. The Spikes gave each other approval, but they had their own standards of approval. Broadly speaking, they approved of anything the people of Madison disapproved. They approved of aggression in any form against anyone not in the gang.

In high school they were despised by the children, particularly by the girls, from more fortunate families. The girls were highly contemptuous of them and treated them as if they were animals. Of course, the Spikes gave the girls some reason to act that way; they were rude and profane. But at any rate, the girls' contempt for them led them to think and speak of women as things to be defiled.

Yet there were times when each of the Spikes, including Frank, secretly wished that he were dressed in a fine suit and taking a girl in a flowered silk dress and high heels to the movies.

When he was sixteen, Frank sauntered up to a girl named June Compton and asked her if she would go to a movie with him. She was vice-president of the junior class at Madison High and when he asked her she looked as if she had been stricken by paralysis. Frank got mad and grabbed her by the shoulders. The girl slapped his face. For some days there was considerable discussion by the other girls about whether she had done the right thing.

This sort of incident, combined with the girls' general contempt for him and his friends and with the anxiety caused him by his mother and grammar school women teachers, led Frank to view women as the principal frustrators of his needs for approval and for avoiding disapproval.

Frank is twenty-two now and he has never had a steady job. The Spikes still hang around together in the evenings. But they don't bother to call themselves "The Spikes" any more. The night Frank raped the girl he was out drinking at a tavern with them. He did not get drunk but he got a little high. Two of his friends had been dancing with a girl who wore a silver bracelet on one ankle. Frank went over and asked her to dance. She refused. She did not refuse because of any particular dislike of Frank, whom she did not even know. She refused simply because her feet hurt. But Frank did not know that. He felt he had been made a fool of in front of his friends. He left the tavern by himself and walked along the dark street. The old aggression was boiling within him.

A girl was hurrying along the other side of the street, beside the park. Frank crossed toward her. She looked at him quickly and then looked straight ahead.

Frank said, "I want to talk to—"

"Get away from me," the girl said. Frank drew his knife, forced her into the park, and raped her.

Let's turn now to the other gentleman in the Madison jail, the sadistic police officer. Sydney Grant is not extreme as sadists go. Of course, he takes great pleasure in rapping prisoners about the head with his night stick and in helping their imaginations to enlarge upon their future punishments. He has been known to surreptitiously invest the prisoners' cell mattresses with a few insects of one kind or another; and on occasion he will oblige if a masochist happens to come his way. But that is about as far as his sadism goes.

Before we continue with Sydney, a word about the relationship between sadism and rape: Rape is, strictly speaking, a form of sadism. Sadism is the broader term and refers to all habits which are intentionally used to hurt and humiliate others, while rape is confined to forced sexual intercourse. This brings up another point. Must sadism always involve sex? No, not necessarily. Sex is often involved but it does not have to be, not in any direct sense at least. In Sydney Grant's case sex is not directly involved.

Obviously Sydney's behavior is motivated primarily by a need to aggress. When he aggresses against others, particularly if they are helpless and in a position where he can humiliate them, Sydney feels a lot better. As in the case of the rapist, Sydney's aggression is due to severe frustration of his needs for approval and for avoiding disapproval. The sadist is, like the rapist, starved for approval, but the sadist does not necessarily look on women as his primary frustrators.

The sadist is an undersocialized individual. Somewhere in his past experience, he has found that hurting and humiliating others has given him relief from the anxiety caused by his strong feelings of aggression. Such behavior satisfies his need to aggress and since he is undersocialized, it causes him few pangs of conscience.

It is somewhat difficult to imagine Sydney Grant as a child. He was, in fact, an exceedingly unhappy one. His mother died as a result of his birth. His father was a poor man but he managed to hire a sort of nurse-housekeeper to look after the boy. The woman took good care of Sydney, but he was not her child and he received little warmth and affection from her.

When Sydney was three years old, his father was killed in an accident at the plant where he worked. The father's relatives did not want to take care of Sydney but they scraped together enough money to put him in a small private home run by a Mrs. Jasper.

There were a dozen children at Mrs. Jasper's, ranging in age from two to thirteen years. Mrs. Jasper looked upon her home as a business, which it was, and she treated the children rather harshly. She paid the two oldest children, a twelve-year-old boy and a thirteen-year-old girl, a small sum each week to look after and discipline the younger children after school hours. The two older children, being frustrated and aggressive, were more concerned with the disciplining than the looking after. They treated the children a few years younger than themselves quite cruelly. This was transmitted down to the youngest children by the seven- and eight-year-olds. Sydney Grant was hurt a lot physically in his first years at Mrs. Jasper's, but the main damage was psychological. He and the other younger children developed the feeling that the world was a cruel place in which there was no one to turn to for protection.

As the years went by the one thing which gave little Sydney pleasure was eating. As Mrs. Jasper often said, "No one can say I don't feed the kids well." There was enough food if not enough love at Mrs. Jasper's and little Sydney grew fat. He was a very homely child and his fat ugliness made him the particular object of ridicule of the other children. When he went to grammar school the ridicule became even greater.

Sydney grew up a vessel of rage. He used to go off by himself down by the railroad tracks. He was least unhappy when he was alone.

Sydney was walking along swinging a stick one day when he came on an old dog which had been hurt. Sydney poked the dog with the stick. The dog moaned. He poked it again. The dog could not stand up and moaned again. Sydney beat the dog to death. In doing so he felt a relief he had never felt before. The pent-up aggression poured out of him with each swing of the stick.

That is not a pretty story but it is important for understanding Sydney. He had never been socialized by anyone and he had no strong feelings of guilt at having beaten the dog to death. All he knew was that he felt better. Throughout his adolescence beating animals secretly became his only pleasure.

When Sydney was in his late teens, he took to hanging around the police station because he liked to watch the policemen bring in the arrested men. He ran errands for the police officers and they grew to like him quite well. They knew nothing of his sadistic tendencies and had no reason not to like him.

Sydney took the examinations for the police force several times and was finally appointed when he was twenty-five. One could not say for certain that his joining the force was motivated by a conscious or unconscious desire to raise his sadistic behavior to the human level. But at any rate Sydney has been on the force for over fifteen years now and his position is such that he can vent his aggression in ways which are not particularly unacceptable to society.

Sydney has never married and has no friends except for a few men on the police force. He lives alone in a house near the center of town on South Street. He owns the house and keeps a colony of cats on hand. When the cells of the Madison jail are empty, howls from Sydney's house are occasionally heard in the night.

Here is a third rather extreme type of aggressor. He sets buildings on fire.

A few minutes before the time when the old Alton warehouse began to burn, a small man went quickly down a Madison side street. It was dusk and the lights were coming on. He looked behind him quickly, kept on moving until he came to the open door of the warehouse. He fired the toylike gun through the open door three noiseless times and moved on.

The gun was the type that is used to fire small darts. The man had it rigged so he could fire the heads of kitchen matches with it. The second match had struck and lighted on the concrete floor of the warehouse. The wooden shavings used for packing were blazing, but the small man did not see that. He was turning the corner and going into the hotel. He went up to his room, quickly took off his coat, drew a chair to the window, and sat down and waited.

Nothing happened.

The little man kept looking down at the warehouse. It stayed the same. He lit a cigarette. Then, faintly, he heard the siren. He smiled and settled back. He watched the warehouse. Smoke began to rise at one side. The siren grew louder, died, then grew louder again, sending a note of urgency through the evening air.

Smoke billowed up into the sky. A fire truck screeched to a halt in the side street. Sirens wailed as the engines converged on the scene. A small red car pulled up and two men jumped out. Flames shot out of the second-story windows of the warehouse. Ladders pointed up into the smoke. Small groups of people gathered.

The small man sat in his hotel room and watched the scene below. He felt as if he were sitting on top of the world. He watched the flames shooting up inside the warehouse windows. The flames were the best part, and the smoke next best. And then the little men in big hats scrambling about like animals.

He was sitting on top of the world watching the warehouse burn and turn to a black skeleton—and all because of him. He felt like yelling at the top of his lungs but he looked behind him at the hotel door and sat still and watched.

The activity below continued. There were smoke, flames, searchlights, ladders, endless upward streams of water, more sirens, more scurrying little men in swept-back hats.

The small man in the hotel room watched with bright eyes. He opened the window a crack and smelled the smoke.

As it turned out the little man was caught, convicted, and sent to prison. He had started four large fires before this one. But this time he was caught because, after watching the fire for hours, he fell into a deep sleep, emotionally exhausted. The next morning the hotel maid knocked on the door several times. Hearing no answer she let herself in with her passkey. She saw the man sleeping and went out.

The maid came back much later and knocked. There was no response, so she let herself in again. The small man was still sleeping. She tried, in vain, to rouse him by shaking his shoulder. The maid grew alarmed and called the desk clerk.

The clerk went up to the man's room and tried to rouse him but could not. He went over to the sleeping man's open suitcase and looked through it. There was the toy gun and with it a box of match heads with the stems broken off. The clerk inspected the gun closely. Then he put it back in the suitcase. He did not connect it with the fire of the night before.

He tried again to rouse the man. Worried that the man might have had a stroke, he went down to the desk and called a doctor.

The small man did not wake up when the doctor arrived. But he was muttering about the beautiful fire and he was smiling in his sleep. As the doctor took the man's pulse, he noticed the gun in the opened suitcase. He went over and examined it and the broken-off match heads. He glanced out the window at the gutted warehouse.

The doctor left the room quietly. He went down to the lobby and told the clerk to call the police.

The small man confessed with some pride to having started the warehouse fire and, in the past year, four other fires as well. His name is Joseph Jaco. He is a fairly young man. He did not grow up in Madison or its vicinity and little is known about his early life. However, certain aspects of his personality and certain facts about his adult years enable one to form some conclusions about why he insists on setting buildings afire.

Like practically all individuals who aggress in unacceptable ways, Jaco is an undersocialized person; his conscience is weak. And over the years, he has been extremely frustrated in his need for approval. He is of average intelligence but has had little education. Sometime during his earlier years he learned the impossible goal of becoming a man of high prestige. He wanted, and still wants, to be that man.

Jaco, having none of the qualities which our society requires of candidates for positions of prestige, has been completely frustrated in his desire to reach his goal. As a consequence he has strong feelings of aggression against the society which he believes has thwarted him at every turn. Starting fires is the way he releases his rage against society. Being undersocialized, the idea of such retaliation does not set off in him the prohibiting anxieties which it would in more socialized individuals.

But why does he resort to arson? Why not some other form of retaliation? Jaco's arsonous behavior began several years ago, soon after he came to Madison. He arrived in Madison practically penniless and took a room in Mrs. Kohn's rooming house. Having worked in laundries before, he soon got a job in the big Madison laundry.

Jaco was severely depressed and he went to work mechanically, day after day. Here he was, thirty years old and working in a laundry. The attainment of his dreams of glory became more remote with each day of his life. But he did not realize that he had little ability which would ever make it possible for him to attain any prestige in the world. He felt, as he had felt for years, that the world was purposely blocking him. He had no friends to turn to.

Late one afternoon, in his room after a day's work at the laundry, Jaco lit a cigarette and tossed the match in the wastebasket. He sat back in his chair and closed his eyes.

Suddenly he looked up. The basket was blazing. He jumped up and then he stopped in the middle of the room. He watched the flames. They darted higher. The curtain on one side of the window caught fire and blazed rapidly. The shade started to burn. The curtain on the other side of the window blazed.

Jaco stood watching. The whole side of the room was ablaze now. He no longer felt tired. He felt fine. Then he remembered that he would be held responsible. He forced himself to go out in the hall, yelling "Fire!"

The man across the hall ran downstairs and called the fire department.

The fire was soon put out without great damage. However, the landlady thought it would be best if Mr. Jaco moved. He moved to another rooming house.

In his room in the evenings, Jaco began to experiment with little fires. He bought some "canned heat" and burned insects over it. He rolled up cellophane into balls and watched, entranced, while they blazed away and shriveled to small black shapes.

Whenever he made a fire and watched the flames, Jaco felt fine. The tense feeling in his stomach temporarily left him. He felt lighter by fifty pounds. He was releasing a little of his aggression and with it a little of the anxiety which it generated in his system.

Now, all day at the laundry he thought about fire. He could close his eyes and see big darting orange flames. The thought came to him that the laundry company was purposely thwarting his ambitions. He decided to set fire to the laundry. In his mind he could see it blazing, and all because of him. He felt good just thinking about it.

Jaco reasoned with some validity that he might be suspected if he started a fire in the laundry. He made a careful, detailed plan to set fire to the laundry's branch on the other end of town. When put into operation, his plan worked perfectly. He stood hidden in the bushes of the park across the street and watched the building burn, while fire trucks raced through the streets.

Soon after that Jaco hit on the idea of using the toy gun. And on four different occasions he pulled its trigger and released against society the aggression which had mounted in him as a result of his frustration at having been unable to attain the prestige and approval he had learned to need.

Chapter 17

SMALLTIMERS

THERE ARE many types who release their aggression in ways which, while rather unacceptable to society at large, are not usually considered criminal. Among these small-timers are the surly type, the poor loser, and the wife beater. Occasionally these three types come wrapped in one bristly, human package, but we will take them one at a time starting with Joe Brock who has a perpetual chip on his shoulder. There is little doubt about it: Joe Brock is a surly, mean cuss.

Joe is the beefy type. He has a red face and his belly is starting to get the best of him; he is young, though, only twenty-four. Joe delivers liquor for the Madison High-Spirits Package Store.

Here is an example of Joe's congeniality. The other day he had parked his truck to make a delivery. He was at the back of the truck and had a case of liquor up on one shoulder. He was struggling to get a second case up on the other shoulder. It was not a question of the weight of the case, it was a question of balancing it as he got it up on his shoulder. A man walking down the street saw that Joe was having difficulty getting the second case up on his shoulder and went over to give him a hand. The man didn't know Joe; he simply had an impulse to give him a hand.

Joe felt the pressure of the man's hands on the case, and he bellowed, "What the hell you doin'?" He slipped the case back on the truck platform and put down the first case.

Joe turned around and stood with his hands on his hips. "Why the hell don't you mind your own damned business?" he said.

The man was dumfounded. He looked as though he couldn't quite believe it.

"What's the matter with you?" Joe bellowed. "Don't you think I can pick up a case of hootch?"

"I was just trying to help you," the man said, reddening. He looked straight at Joe, shook his head, and walked away.

"I ought to have bust you in the snoot," Joe called after him and then said to no one in particular, "Meddlin' bastard."

Well, that's typical of Joe Brock. That genial bulk of his is loaded with feelings of aggression.

Joe Brock's parents were a pretty rough pair. Their income was low but they liked to live high. Joe's father was an iceman by occupation but his business was not a large one since his schedule was rather irregular. Sometimes he made his rounds in the morning, sometimes he made them in the afternoon, and sometimes he did not make them at all. His customers were mainly those who, failing to have the funds to pay for ice, could not afford to deal with icemen of greater dependability.

The Brocks lived on the west end of town just off Black Row. The houses were not better than those in Black Row but there were no Negroes in the block. This made all the difference in the world to Joe's father. At the beer tavern he frequented when he was contemplating making his rounds, he would speak of "them black bastards" and explain to all who would listen that he "would not deliver a piece of ice to any black bastard in this world, not if he was to pay a dollar a pound for it."

Joe's mother was frequently of the opinion that "life is too God-damned dull." She liked a party now and then and never tired of pressing her mate to take her out and have some fun. Seldom did she meet with overly strong resistance to her wishes.

It cannot be said that Joe, the Brocks' only offspring, was left to shift entirely for himself. At times, when the Brock parents were out on the town, this was true. But in the main, Joe was brought up with enough guidance and consistency of reward and punishment to keep him from later developing criminal habits. The Brocks socialized the boy after their fashion, if not too well.

When he was sixteen, Joe had a physique like a heavyweight and he was a good-looking boy. "With a built like that, he could be a champeen," his father took to declaring. The elder Brock took the boy down to Max's Gym and asked his cronies there to teach Joe the ropes. Joe could really punch but he had one little difficulty:

his feet often got in each other's way. He simply could not control them.

Joe trained steadily at Max's Gym for several years. To put it briefly, he was hopeless. He had the build, he could punch, but he was off balance more of the time than he was not. At his father's insistence, Max, the local promoter, arranged a few fights for him. Joe managed to lose them all.

When Joe was nineteen he started delivering for the Madison High-Spirits Package Store, a place of business with which the elder Brock was not totally unfamiliar. Joe has been there for five years now. He still goes down to Max's Gym on his day off and works out. He really looks good standing up there hitting the punching bag. But when he steps into the ring and starts moving around he looks like a clumsy elephant walking upright on a field of cannon balls.

Joe's need for a place in the sun has been quite frustrated by his failure to rise in the ring. Thus he is aggressive and tries to work that aggression off at every chance. He threatens to back up his surly ways with his fists and sometimes does. He is the successful fighter—outside the ring. Usually he can keep his feet untangled long enough to land one good blow on his surprised target. Of course, not only does Joe release his aggression in this way; he also gains a feeling of approval for playing the role of a tough guy. But all in all, his surliness and readiness to "bust him in the snoot" are escape valves for his strong feelings of aggression. He gets particularly incensed at anyone who, like the man who tried to help him with the case of liquor, implies that he is something less than well coordinated. After all, that has been the major cause of his frustration.

Another small-time aggressor is the poor loser. A pretty fair example of this type is Bill Bancroft, as pleasant a fellow as you're likely to meet—when he's not losing. Bill lives out in Beauty Hills and is a rising young lawyer. But the last time the Bancrofts and the Dodges played bridge together Bill was feeling something less than pleasant at the end of the first rubber.

Jean Bancroft was about to add up the score. "I can see right now, without even adding it up, that you've won this rubber, Helen," Jean said.

Helen Dodge said, "We hardly ever win. It's just luck. You were way ahead of us until that last hand."

Jean Bancroft finished adding the score and put down the pencil. "Fifteen hundred and sixty to seven-twenty. We ought to take a few lessons from you," she said to Helen and Jim Dodge.

Bill Bancroft had been standing looking into the fireplace and now he wheeled around.

"You mean you ought to, you damned fool," he said to his wife.

"Bill, please—" Jean said.

"Now, Bill, we were just lucky this time," Jim Dodge said.

"Lucky, hell. You were bound to win, with me saddled with an idiot," Bill said. His face looked pinker than usual.

"Bill, please," Jean Bancroft said. "Get Jim and Helen a drink and we'll—"

"If you and Helen didn't gab all the time, you might be able to keep track of what's been played."

"Now, old man, what does it matter?" Jim Dodge said. "It's just a game. It doesn't—"

"It may not matter to you but it matters to me," Bill said. "I don't mind losing but I'll be damned if I like to lose simply because of the stupidity of my brilliant wife."

"Bill, please. Go and get Jim and Helen a drink," Jean said.

"Just a friendly game, old man," Jim Dodge said.

Helen Dodge was moving toward the door. "We really have to be going," she said.

"Yes, we've got to be going," Jim said and started quickly for the coats in the hall closet.

"Oh, no, don't go yet. Stay and play another rubber. It's still early," Jean Bancroft said.

"No, really dear, we must," Helen Dodge said. "The baby-sitter—"

"Yes, the baby-sitter," Jim Dodge said, giving his wife her coat.

Bill Bancroft seemed to have disappeared.

"Good night, Bill," Jim Dodge called.

No answer.

"Good night, dear," Helen Dodge said to Jean. "It's been a lot of fun."

The Dodges wasted no time in leaving.

As soon as they had left, Bill Bancroft came out of the kitchen.

"You damn fool," he said to his wife, Jean. "Can't you ever learn when not to double?" He went on at great length.

It's getting a little hard for the Bancrofts to find anyone to play bridge with. Bill is always like this when he loses at bridge or anything else. If his wife is around, he takes it out on her. He knows he can get away with it.

What makes him act this way? Why does he take losing so seriously? Doesn't he realize that his behavior only leads others to disapprove of him?

Well, losing at any game implies definite disapproval to Bill much more than it does to the average person. To him, winning stands for approval and losing stands for disapproval. In a way, this is the case with most people, but with Bill the whole thing is exaggerated.

The reasons for this go back to Bill's school days. Bill was sent away to a military academy when he was thirteen. There was tremendous emphasis on competition there, on athletic competition in particular.

Bill was hazed unmercifully as were all new cadets. The way to prove one's self at the military academy was to excel in athletics or in the various military competitions. Having come at a later age than many of the cadets, Bill was at a disadvantage in military competition. Therefore, during his years at the military academy Bill tried to prove himself in sports and he often succeeded.

At the academy, to win meant real glory and to lose meant just as real ignominy. There was no such thing as a pat on the back for a game well lost. So there became incorporated into Bill's personality the ideas that winning stood for strong approval and that losing stood for strong disapproval. Learned reactions were set up in Bill's nervous system between losing and a feeling of disapproval and between winning and a feeling of approval.

Today those conditioned reactions still operate in Bill. When he wins, he feels fine. But when he loses, the old feeling of disapproval comes over him strongly. He feels frustrated and aggression rises within him. He can't control it. It is a conditioned reaction and he does not recognize it for what it is. He always finds some way to rationalize the situation—his wife didn't do that or she didn't do this—so that he feels justified in venting his aggression.

A third small-time aggressor is the wife beater. He's not always such a small-timer, come to think of it. At any rate, he usually operates on a little larger scale than the poor loser. The wife beater we have in mind is one Richard Collins, whom we mentioned briefly at the beginning of this book. Approximately once a month Richard loses control of himself, attacks of rage come over him, and he beats his wife quite thoroughly. His most recent outburst ended with an unsuccessful attempt to shove her in the furnace.

Between periods of such aggression, Collins runs his book and stationery store with what seems to be a benign hand. He appears to be a mild and pleasant man.

Collins is about forty years old now. As a very young man, twenty years ago, he was rather starry-eyed. He wanted to be a novelist, and he was sure he would be. He had so much to say, he felt, and all he had to do was put it on paper. He would be able to give his thoughts to countless others and fame would come to him.

At that time, Richard Collins met his future wife Hazel. Little did he look upon her then as a monthly punching bag. He was entranced. She thought the little he had written was wonderful, and so he thought she was wonderful.

They made their plans. They would marry and, with the little money which had been left Richard, they would open a small bookstore. They would take turns tending the store. That would give him time to write. She would like that, Hazel said, because she had always liked good books.

They were married, and they opened the store. They sold stationery and gifts as well as books. It was a pretty little shop with curtains at the windows. Business was slow at first but soon things started to go well.

Richard stayed home in the mornings to write while Hazel tended the store. Then in the afternoon he would tend the store while Hazel did the housework. But somehow or other Richard couldn't seem to accomplish much in the mornings. What he wrote never seemed to do justice to the wonderful ideas which had floated in and out of his mind for years. Then in the afternoon when he was in the store there always seemed to be problems created by what seemed to him to be Hazel's inefficiency in the morning. How could she expect him to accomplish anything at home in the mornings, he wanted to know, when he had to worry about what she was failing to do at the store?

This went on for some time, Richard rationalizing that his inability to write was due to Hazel's failure to do her part at the store. The real trouble was that what he had to say was only hazily formed in his mind, and that he expected too much too soon and would not admit to himself that he needed a few years of practice.

Then Hazel became pregnant and eventually had to stop working in the store. This made it necessary for Richard to spend all his time there. He felt that the situation made it impossible for him to write at all. While he did not tell his wife, he blamed her for having the baby and so making it impossible for him to achieve his goal. He rationalized things to the point where he saw his failure as completely her fault.

As time went on, Richard increasingly though unconsciously used the store as an escape. He kept it open in the evenings although few customers came in then. He grew fussier and fussier about just how the merchandise should be displayed. He convinced himself completely that fate and Hazel had conspired against him and made it impossible for him to realize his ambition to write. There were periods during the day when business was very slack and he could have written at length. But he was always too occupied doing unnecessary things around the store.

Richard felt with increasing severity the frustration of his need for approval because of his failure to become a famous writer. Here he was, the keeper of a small store. It was not what he had planned at all. He was a reasonably socialized person, but beneath his easy-going exterior feelings of aggression mounted and had no outlet.

It may seem that in cases of aggressive types the frustration behind their aggression results, with rather extreme regularity, from their failure to achieve the positions in society which they once set as their goals. However, that is the way things are; behind aggression often lie unfulfilled dreams of a place in the social sun.

Over the years Richard Collins' feelings of aggression continued to mount. Increasingly he saw—part consciously and part unconsciously—his wife, Hazel, as the cause of his inability to fulfill his dreams. One night when he came home from the store, Hazel was extremely upset. Their child, now a girl of eight, was doing very poorly in school. The teacher had asked Hazel to come to the school for a conference about it, which Hazel had done that afternoon. Hazel was extremely upset at the idea of their child not being a bright student. So was Richard when Hazel told him about it. One thing led to another, and then Hazel said to him, "If you'd ever take any interest in the child, if you'd ever do anything but sit down in that store trying to escape from everything, maybe this wouldn't have happened. Maybe a lot of things would have been different."

This was too much for Richard Collins. It struck a deep, sore spot in him because it was the truth. He *was* escaping at the store. But at the same time, he had come to see his wife as the cause of his failure. He struck her across the face. He struck her several times. She fell down and he stopped.

He had never done such a thing before and his wife was dumfounded. So was he. After he regained control of himself, he told her how sorry he was and asked her to forgive him, which she did.

Six months later much the same thing happened. Since then, Richard's outbursts of aggression against his wife have become more frequent, occurring perhaps every month. The aggression builds up in him and is tripped off by some small thing which she unintentionally says or does and which Richard interprets as criticism. She seldom actually criticizes him. However, he has this periodic need for an excuse to release his aggression, and he really believes that she is the primary cause of his frustration. So he unconsciously seizes on one thing or another which she says or does and misinterprets it. Afterward he feels somewhat guilty and tells her how sorry he is. Then in a month or so, his feelings of aggression become stronger than the threat of his wife's-and his own disapproval and he lashes out at her again.

Chapter 18

A CONCLUDING WORD

LOOKING BACK on the characters in this book—the approval seekers, the disapproval avoiders and the aggressors—one can see a number of themes recurring. First, the need for approval and for avoiding disapproval are learned by individuals in early life. As children they associate the approval of their parents with satisfaction of their needs and they associate their parents' disapproval with frustration of their needs. People learn to want approval because it stands for satisfaction, and they learn to want to avoid disapproval because it stands for frustration.

Habits are learned in an effort to satisfy these needs for approval and for avoiding disapproval. This learning usually begins in early life, but it may occur in later years as well. Most frequently, people learn habits by imitating others—their parents, schoolmates, and adult associates. Thus, the particular behavior they learn in order to satisfy their needs is largely a result of the influences of the people who have made up their past environments.

Sometimes, however, the habits people learn for trying to satisfy their needs for approval and for avoiding disapproval fail to do the job. When this is the case, a consequent feeling of frustration leads to a need to aggress. The ways in which people behave in their attempts to satisfy this need to aggress are also learned. Again, their behavior is in great part a result of the influences of the individuals who have made up their past environments, particularly their parents. People whose parents have overemphasized socially accepted behavior, will be inclined to aggress against themselves, while those who have been undersocialized will be likely to aggress against others. If, however, their parents have socialized them well, but not too well, they will have learned habits for releasing aggression which are neither harmful to themselves nor particularly unacceptable to their society.

In summary, three of the chief needs behind human behavior in modern society are the learned needs for gaining approval, for avoiding disapproval, and for the instinctive need to aggress which arises when either of the former, or any other need, is frustrated. The ways in which people try to satisfy these needs are learned as a result of the conscious or unconscious influences of the people, particularly the parents, in their past environments. In large part, humans are creatures of environmental circumstance. And if we have some insight into why this is so, we may be able to better comprehend not only others but ourselves as well.

Obviously living people are infinitely more complex than any of the characters in this book. The sketches drawn here are at best only snapshots of one side or another of multi-sided personalities. Also the causative factors related to human behavior are many times more complex than presented here. There is, to be sure, more behind any individual's behavior than the needs for gaining approval, avoiding disapproval, and for releasing aggression. However, any scheme of explanation must simplify; otherwise it would be just as confusing as the actual phenomena it attempts to explain. I have selected the factors which seem to me most important for understanding the behavior of people in modern society. My hope is that such simplification will lead to an increased understanding of why people act as they do.

THE END

Why Do Married Couples Cheat?

a noted psychiatrist discusses the causes and cures of a major social problem in a thoughtful and fascinating book.

UNFAITHFUL

former title: Marital Infidelity

by Dr. Frank S. Caprio

Member of the American Psychiatric Association

Some of the vital questions this book answers are:

How does the sexual relationship in marriage affect infidelity?

Is infidelity a neurosis?

What is the difference between normal and neurotic jealousy?

How should a wife handle "the other woman"?

Is it wise to confess infidelity to one's partner in marriage?

> *". . . frank and courageous . . . a fine, original contribution to the layman's understanding."*
>
> **Dr. Rose N. Franzblau**

d449

ONLY 50¢ WHEREVER PAPERBACK BOOKS ARE SOLD

If your dealer is sold out, send only 50¢ plus 10¢ for postage and handling to Crest Books, Fawcett Publications, Inc., Greenwich, Conn. Please order by number and title. If five or more books are ordered, no postage or handling charge is necessary. No Canadian orders.

From CREST and PREMIER—

BOOKS FOR PEOPLE WHO WANT MORE OUT OF LIFE

Discover Your SELF   Premier d86—50¢

by Dr. Stephan Lackner—An outstanding practical guide to auto-analysis that can help you to discover the talents you have, the person you are and the person you can be.

How to Live with Yourself and Like It   Premier d71—50¢

Former title: The Art of Human Relations

by Harry Clay Lindgren—An exciting guide to self-understanding that will help you become a happier, more successful and more interesting person.

How to Invest Safely and for Profit   Crest d376—50¢

by Adolph Suehsdorf—If you really want to know how to make money in the stock market, this book is the best investment you will ever make.

25 Magic Steps to Word Power   Crest d356—50¢

by Wilfred Funk—A noted lexicographer, the creator of the Reader's Digest feature *It Pays to Increase Your Word Power*, shows how word power is the key to successful living and offers an easy, entertaining way to increase your vocabulary day by day.

The Practical Way to a Better Memory   Premier d59—50¢

Former title: How to Remember

by Dr. Bruno Furst—The world's greatest memory expert offers a simple and effective blueprint for teaching yourself to remember facts, figures and faces, sharpen your power of observation, learn foreign languages quickly, develop your powers of concentration, and speak in public without stage fright.

If your dealer is sold out, send only cover price plus 10¢ each for postage and handling to Crest and Premier Books, Fawcett Publications, Inc., Greenwich, Conn. Please order by number and title. If five or more books are ordered, no postage or handling charge is necessary. No Canadian orders.